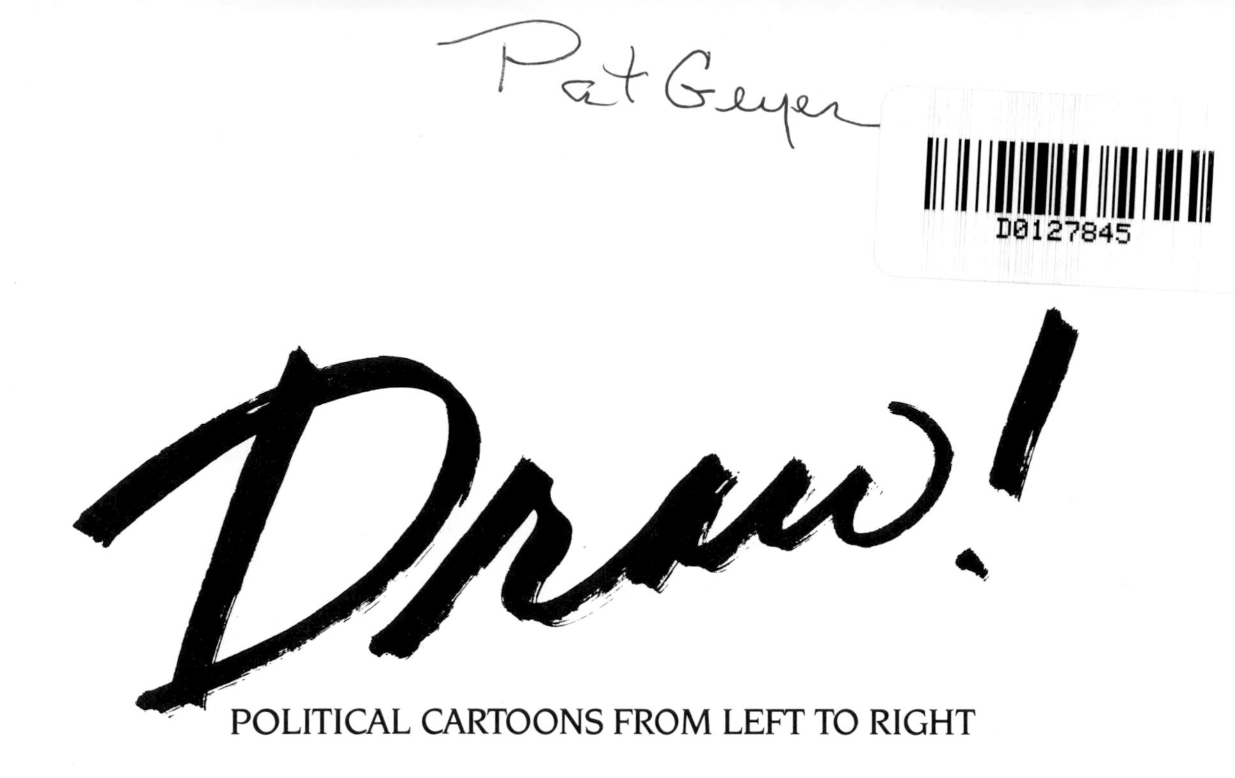

POLITICAL CARTOONS FROM LEFT TO RIGHT

Text by Stacey Bredhoff
Exhibition Curator

Foreword by Don W. Wilson
Archivist of the United States

An exhibition
at the National Archives
commemorating
the 200th anniversary
of the Bill of Rights

June 14, 1991–August 31, 1992

Library of Congress
Cataloging-in-Publication Data

Bredhoff, Stacey, 1955-
Draw! : political cartoons from left to right / by Stacey Bredhoff.
p. cm.
Catalog of an exhibition held at the National Archives and Records Administration from June 14, 1991-Aug. 1992.
Includes bibliographical references.
ISBN 0-911333-85-1 (s/c) : $7.95
1. United States — Politics and government — Caricatures and cartoons — Exhibitions. 2. American wit and humor, Pictorial — Exhibitions. 3. United States. National Archives and Records Administration — Exhibitions. I. United States. National Archives and Records Administration. II. Title.
E183.B854 1991 91-2559
320.973'0207 — dc20 CIP

1991

Designed by Janice Hargett, National Archives

CONTENTS

The National Archives preserves and makes available for research the permanently valuable records of the federal government from its beginnings. Although the National Archives was not established until 1934, its major holdings date back to 1774. The National Archives is a national resource, with facilities in 16 states. These include 8 Presidential libraries, 12 regional archives, and 14 records centers.

The records of the nation's civil, military, and diplomatic activities are here. They capture the sweep of America's past: slave ship manifests and the Emancipation Proclamation; journals of polar expeditions and photographs of Dust Bowl farmers; Indian treaties that made transitory promises and the Louisiana Purchase Treaty, which doubled the territory of the young Republic; and the records of all our wars and conflicts. In all, more than 4 billion pieces of paper, 6 million still pictures, 111,827 motion pictures, 187,243 sound and video recordings, 1,908,477 maps and charts, 2,079,380 architectural and engineering drawings, and 8,939,269 aerial photographs are held in trust for the American people by the National Archives.

The exhibition and catalogue, "DRAW! Political Cartoons From Left to Right," are supported by a grant from Philip Morris Companies, Inc.

FOREWORD

This year marks the 200th anniversary of the ratification of one of the most marvelous instruments of the free world. On December 15, 1791, Virginia became the 11th state to ratify 10 of 12 proposed amendments to the Constitution, which became known as the Bill of Rights.

This document is the culmination of the 17-year struggle of a new nation to create a unique political testament. The Declaration of Independence was a stirring call to overthrow the bonds of tyranny and to proclaim the rights of life, liberty, and the pursuit of happiness. The Constitution gave the revolutionary words of the Declaration a framework and the force of law. The Bill of Rights enumerated, with eloquent simplicity and unmistakable fervor, the basic rights of personal liberty.

Through the years, the meaning of these documents has evolved, gaining new force while eroding old prejudices. Indeed, they could be called the instruments of the American enlightenment, for they enunciated the noblest goals but recognized the imperfections of governments. The legislators who drafted the Constitution in Philadelphia and those who ratified the Bill of Rights in 11 states anticipated a changing society. Many of the expanded freedoms we take for granted today have come to us through the courts in the last 50 years; those guaranteed by the first amendment are no exception.

The purpose of this exhibition is to give visual expression to the freedom of speech. The cartoons in this exhibition range from the merely prickly to the wickedly satirical. Their range is truly reflective of the healthy state of political debate in this country. They serve to remind us that the first amendment is alive and well in our society — and this is, indeed, a cause for celebration.

As the nation approached this bicentennial commemoration, we at the National Archives wanted to use this opportunity to create a greater understanding of the Bill of Rights and its relevance today. To do this effectively, we needed the help of the private sector.

Of the many corporations contacted, only the Philip Morris Companies agreed to underwrite this exhibition. In addition, the Companies underwrote the publication of an annotated reproduction of the Bill of Rights, which was made available, free of charge, to more than 4 million people. With appropriated funds alone, the National Archives could never have hoped to reach such a broad audience.

This support has garnered some criticism of which I am keenly aware. The debate is, in my view, a perfect example of why the first amendment is so crucial to the survival of our democratic society. This debate has been given voice in Congress, in the press, and in a variety of other forums. I welcome it. I would hope, however, that critics would remember that the freedom of speech provision of the first amendment is unrestricted and that corporations as well as individuals are protected by it.

Through their support of this exhibition and free copies of the Bill of Rights, the Philip Morris Companies are serving the public interest. In no manner is the National Archives serving them or their products. The public-spirited efforts of private enterprise should be encouraged, for it is only through the forging of public and private partnerships that the vitality of American culture can be broadly appreciated. This partnership must not be stilled. If it is, the first amendment itself will be the victim.

Don W. Wilson
Archivist of the United States

ACKNOWLEDGMENTS

The exhibition "**DRAW! Political Cartoons From Left to Right**" was developed by the Office of Public Programs, National Archives and Records Administration, under the direction of Linda N. Brown, Edith M. James, and Emily W. Soapes.

This publication was designed by Janice Hargett. Special appreciation is extended to David Sutton, who designed the exhibition while on the staff of the National Archives Exhibits Branch and generously continued to provide crucial assistance through the production phase, in spite of a career move. We are also grateful to James D. Zeender, registrar of the exhibition, and to Lisa Auel, Bruce Bustard, and Stephen Estrada of the Exhibits Branch.

This project could not have been accomplished without the assistance and cooperation of many National Archives staff members within the Office of Presidential Libraries. John Fawcett, Patrick Borders, and Douglas Thurman helped to coordinate the efforts of a great many individuals at the Presidential libraries. Special appreciation is extended to Joan Maske and Maureen Harding at the Herbert Hoover Library; Alycia Vivona and Tex Parks at the Franklin D. Roosevelt Library; Patricia Dorsey, Mark Beveridge, and Clay Bauske at the Harry S. Truman Library; Dennis Medina and Marion Kamm at the Dwight D. Eisenhower Library; Allan Goodrich at the John Fitzgerald Kennedy Library; Patricia Burchfield and Gary Yarrington at the Lyndon Baines Johnson Library; Walton Owen of the Nixon Presidential Materials Staff; Jane Isaacs, Scott Houting, and Jim Kratsas at the Gerald R. Ford Museum; Sylvia Naguib and Nancy Hassett at the Jimmy Carter Library; and Sherrie Fletcher and Rod Soubers of the Reagan Presidential Materials Staff. We also appreciate the help of Ed McCarter of the Still Picture Branch, Office of the National Archives.

Angie Spicer of the Office of the National Archives and Andrea Peterson of the Office of Presidential Libraries provided crucial assistance in the compilation of this book. Catherine Nicholson and other members of the Document Conservation Branch aided in the preparation of the exhibition and catalog through their work with the drawings themselves, as did Earl MacDonald and other staff members in the National Archives Photographic Laboratory. Jill D. Brett, Public Affairs Officer of the National Archives, reviewed countless drafts of the manuscript, offering helpful editorial revisions each step of the way. Sandra Tilley and Mary C. Ryan of the Publications Division, Office of Public Programs, proofread the manuscript with great care and patience.

Bernard Reilly, head of the Curatorial Section, Prints and Photographs Division at the Library of Congress, turned his expert's eye and mind to the manuscript and offered invaluable suggestions and counsel. Dr. Stephen E. Ambrose, Director of the Eisenhower Center at the University of New Orleans, also reviewed the manuscript with his own wealth of knowledge and contributed important advice. Cartoonist Mike Peters of the *Dayton Daily News* provided important insights into the nature of his work through a series of telephone conversations. We are grateful to them for their unique contributions and generosity with their time.

We appreciate the generosity of the many working cartoonists and private collectors who have made the original drawings available for this project. Their names are listed in the captions within this book.

Finally, we are most grateful to all the political cartoonists who exercise their first amendment rights to the benefit of us all.

Stacey Bredhoff
Exhibits Branch, National Archives

This book is dedicated to the first amendment of the United States Constitution:

Congress shall make no law respecting an establishment of religion, or prohibiting the free exercise thereof; or abridging the freedom of speech, or of the press; or the right of the people peaceably to assemble, and to petition the Government for a redress of grievances.

INTRODUCTION

Unrestrained debate on issues of common concern is a crucial element in the formula for successful self-government. In an open society, political debates are heard everywhere. The first amendment to the U.S. Constitution, which guarantees free speech and freedom of the press, fosters this open exchange of ideas. Protected by the first amendment, Americans from all walks of life are free to form opinions, share ideas, and influence each other's views without fear of recrimination.

The first amendment to the Constitution and the nine subsequent amendments are known collectively as the Bill of Rights. They embody the principle of personal freedom that fueled the American Revolution and have been part of the Constitution since December 15, 1791. In commemoration of the 200th anniversary of the Bill of Rights, the National Archives has developed an exhibition and catalog that celebrate a unique vehicle for political debate: the political cartoon.

There is nothing subtle about American political cartoons. They are unabashed expressions of individual viewpoints. On the editorial pages of our newspapers and magazines, political cartoonists air their views with no pretense of fairness and with no apologies. Any issue or any person who captures public attention is fair game for the political cartoonist. Although many political cartoons display great humor, cartoonists are actually engaged in the very serious business of self-government. With no holds barred, they contribute their unique combination of talents — artistry, humor, and insight — to the steady stream of competing ideas that characterizes a free society.

"DRAW! Political Cartoons From Left to Right" is an exhibition and catalog of some 130 original drawings for cartoons that reflect public sentiment during the last 120 years. The selection of cartoons for the exhibition reflects, in large part, the strengths and weaknesses of the various collections of the National Archives. Research in the collections did not reveal a comprehensive history of political cartoons. In the process of developing the exhibition, however, certain persistent concerns of American life did emerge as themes.

Although the names and faces of the people depicted in the cartoons change as often as the headlines, the underlying themes remain surprisingly constant. They transcend the specific facts of the situations portrayed to offer up a deeper message about the values of the American people and the nature of our political system. The exhibition and catalog are organized according to these general subjects: war and peace; political corruption; Presidential caricatures; the race for the White House; the balance of power; and other domestic issues, including civil rights, national security, the economy, and the right to privacy. One of the goals of this organization is to allow the drawings to explain each other with a minimum of interpretive text.

In the section entitled "Balance of Power," for example, cartoons from the Hoover, Franklin Roosevelt, Eisenhower, Ford, and Carter administrations all show the President and the Congress in conflict with each other. One need not be familiar with the specific facts of each situation depicted to appreciate that these cartoons reveal the tension inherent in the system of checks and balances among the three branches of government.

Similarly, in the section on political corruption, cartoons relating to the Teapot Dome scandal of 1924, the Watergate affair that dominated American politics in the early 1970s,

"A Presidential Touch"
by Cy Hungerford, appeared in the *Pittsburgh Post-Gazette*, January 17, 1957
Dwight D. Eisenhower Library, National Archives
Reprinted through the courtesy of Cy Hungerford and the *Pittsburgh Post-Gazette*

"Another Boundary Dispute!"
by Walter J. Enright, appeared in the *Evening World*, ca. 1929–30
Herbert Hoover Library, National Archives

"And When Did You First Notice We Weren't Listening?"
by Hy Rosen, appeared in the *Albany Times Union*, April 13, 1975
Gerald R. Ford Museum, National Archives
Reprinted through the courtesy of Hy Rosen

and the financial scandals uncovered at the Department of Housing and Urban Development in 1989 are juxtaposed. They all affirm the conviction that no individual is above the law.

The work of Thomas Nast, often described as the father of the American political cartoon, hastened the downfall of the corrupt Tammany Ring, New York City's Democratic Party's political machine that swindled millions of dollars from the public in the early 1870s. As head of the Tammany Ring, "Boss" Tweed was Nast's prime target. A succession of Nast drawings appeared in *Harper's Weekly*, relentlessly lambasting "Boss" Tweed and his cronies. When Tweed

"Who Stole the People's Money? Do Tell. 'Twas Him" by Thomas Nast, appeared in *Harper's Weekly*, August 17, 1871
Office of Public Programs, National Archives

saw the cartoon "Who Stole the People's Money?" he is supposed to have said, "Let's stop them damn pictures. . . . I don't care so much what the papers say about me — my constituents can't read; but damn it, they can see pictures!" Eventually, Tweed was brought to trial and sentenced to prison. He was well aware of the power of the political cartoon. The pictures haven't stopped yet.

A Note on the Collections

Unless otherwise noted, the cartoons in the exhibition are original drawings from the National Archives. They are a small sampling from the cartoon collections held by the eight Presidential libraries, the Nixon and Reagan Presidential Materials Staffs, and the National Archives Still Picture Branch. The Presidential libraries preserve the records of Presidents Hoover, Franklin Roosevelt, Truman, Eisenhower, Kennedy, Lyndon Johnson, Ford, and Carter and are operated and maintained by the National Archives.

The presence of the cartoons in these collections attest to the affection that many of the cartoonists felt for the people they lampooned: most of the drawings were gifts from the cartoonists to the Presidents. Many of them bear respectful inscriptions from the artists that belie the irreverence of the drawings. With the exception of the cartoon collection at the Johnson Library, the gifts were unsolicited. They were presented by cartoonists or their family members to Presidents or their family members, or to a Presidential library. Although some Presidents would, on occasion, ask a cartoonist for a specific drawing that appeared in a newspaper, only President Johnson had a systematic, deliberate collecting practice.

"The Harried Piano Player"
by Joseph Parrish, appeared in the *Chicago Tribune*, 1948
Harry S. Truman Library, National Archives

"Gee . . . I Feel Like I Understand Those Cartoonists Much Better Now. . . . Somebody Count the Silverware"
by Jim Borgman, the *Cincinnati Enquirer*, 1986
Reagan Presidential Materials Staff, National Archives
Reprinted through the courtesy of Jim Borgman/ *The Cincinnati Enquirer*

"President Hoover Gets a Great Kick Out of His Cartoon Collection"
by Clifford K. Berryman, appeared in the *Washington Evening Star*, October 1932
Herbert Hoover Library, National Archives
© 1932, *The Washington Post*, reprinted with permission

"A Brave Man"
by Cy Hungerford, appeared in the *Pittsburgh Post-Gazette*, not dated
Lyndon Baines Johnson Library, National Archives
Reprinted through the courtesy of Cy Hungerford and the *Pittsburgh Post-Gazette*

"That Man in the White House"
by Robert Zschiesche, appeared in the *Greensboro Daily News*, September 7, 1967
Lyndon Baines Johnson Library, National Archives
Reprinted through the courtesy of Robert Zschiesche

"We've Grown Accustomed To Your Face"
by Frank Tyger, appeared in the *Trenton Times*, not dated
Lyndon Baines Johnson Library, National Archives
Reprinted through the courtesy of the *Trenton Times*

President Johnson and the turbulent times of his Presidency inspired a great number of political cartoons.

In 1964 President Johnson assigned to an assistant the task of locating and soliciting original drawings for cartoons that said something about the activities of his administration. The cartoons represent all kinds of viewpoints — those critical of the President, as well as those supportive of him. The result of this aggressive collection policy and the extraordinary generosity of the cartoonists is a collection of some 3,800 original cartoons

"Et Tu, Y'All?"
by Ken Alexander, appeared in the *San Francisco Examiner*, 1960s
Lyndon Baines Johnson Library, National Archives
Reprinted through the courtesy of Ken Alexander and the *San Francisco Examiner*

at the Johnson Library, which accounts for slightly more than half of the total number of cartoons held by all eight Presidential libraries combined.

Among the holdings of the National Archives Still Picture Branch are 850 political cartoons that were in the picture files of longtime FBI director J. Edgar Hoover. The cartoons, collected for display purposes, focus on issues relating to the FBI, J. Edgar Hoover, law and order, sabotage, and communism.

"Sees All—Knows All!"
by Fred Graf, appeared in the *Nassau Daily Review*, March 8, 1949
Still Picture Branch, National Archives

All of the cartoon collections mentioned here are part of the holdings of the National Archives and are available for research at the following locations:

Herbert Hoover Library
West Branch, IA

Franklin D. Roosevelt Library
Hyde Park, NY

Harry S. Truman Library
Independence, MO

Dwight D. Eisenhower Library
Abilene, KS

John Fitzgerald Kennedy Library
Boston, MA

Lyndon Baines Johnson Library
Austin, TX

Gerald R. Ford Museum
Grand Rapids, MI

Jimmy Carter Library
Atlanta, GA

Reagan Presidential Materials Staff
Los Angeles, CA

Nixon Presidential Materials Staff
Alexandria, VA

National Archives Still Picture Branch
Washington, DC

WAR AND PEACE

Public opinion plays an important role in an effective national defense. Along with military might, a strong defense requires that people have faith in their leaders and in their nation's ideals and current policies.

"Come On In, I'll Treat You Right. I Used To Know Your Daddy"
by C. D. Batchelor, appeared in the *New York Daily News*, April 25, 1936
Pulitzer Prize Collection, Columbia University

During the 1930s an antiwar spirit prevailed in the United States. Created less than 20 years after the end of World War I, this cartoon portrays war as a seductress who could lure yet another generation of Europeans into a bloody conflict. Batchelor won a Pulitzer Prize in 1937 for this drawing.

"Come on in. I'll treat you right. I used to know your daddy."

"The Misfit"
by Edwin Marcus, appeared in the *New York Times*, 1933
Library of Congress, Prints and Photographs Division
Reprinted through the courtesy of Donald E. Marcus

In the early 1930s Hitler was portrayed as a comic figure. It wasn't until the late 1930s and 1940s that he appeared as a threatening symbol of domination and evil.

WORLD WAR II

Once engaged, the United States waged World War II with the full support of the American people. The cartoons produced during World War II show little criticism of the U.S. government; cartoonists reserved their venom for the enemy.

ANOTHER GOOD SOLDIER –

"Another Good Soldier"
by Rube Goldberg, March 9, 1942
Franklin D. Roosevelt Library, National Archives
Reprinted through the courtesy of King Features Syndicate, Inc.

World War II bound Americans together in a common goal. Civilians enthusiastically participated in the war effort in many ways.

MON. MAR. 9. 1942

"A Tree Grows in Berlin"
by Daniel Robert Fitzpatrick, appeared in the St. Louis
Post Dispatch, August 17, 1944
Victoria Schuck Collection at the John Fitzgerald
Kennedy Library, National Archives
Fitzpatrick in the *St. Louis Post-Dispatch*

"The Harvest"
by Daniel Robert Fitzpatrick, appeared in the *St. Louis Post-Dispatch*, November 27, 1938
Victoria Schuck Collection at the John Fitzgerald Kennedy Library, National Archives
Fitzpatrick in the *St. Louis Post-Dispatch*

"Fresh, spirited American troops, flushed with victory are bringing in thousands of hungry, ragged, battle weary prisoners." (News item)

"'Fresh, spirited American troops, flushed with victory, are bringing in thousands of hungry, ragged, battle-weary prisoners. . . .' (*News Item*)"
by Bill Mauldin, United Feature Syndicate, Inc., 1944
Pulitzer Prize Collection, Columbia University
Reprinted with permission of Bill Mauldin and *Bill Mauldin's Army*, © 1944, Presidio Press

Sgt. Bill Mauldin produced cartoons for the Army newspaper, *Stars and Stripes*, while with the infantry in Europe. He created characters Willie and Joe, the war-weary, mud-splattered foot soldiers who gave voice to thousands of American fighting men. In this drawing, Mauldin commented on the rosy accounts of the war that appeared in the American press. He wrote, "After a few days of battle, the victorious Yank who has been sweeping ahead doesn't look any prettier than the sullen superman he captures." In 1945 Mauldin received a Pulitzer Prize for this drawing.

"Who's Pearl Harbor?"
by Lee Judge, appeared in the *Kansas City Times*, August 7, 1985
Harry S. Truman Library, National Archives
Reprinted through the courtesy of Lee Judge and the *Kansas City Times*

"Class of '45"
by Bill Mauldin, October 16, 1967
Dwight D. Eisenhower Library, National Archives
Reprinted with permission of Bill Mauldin

Twenty-two years after the end of the war, cartoonist Bill Mauldin revisited his wartime creation and made a gift to President Eisenhower.

For an entire generation of Americans the events of World War II, both at home and abroad, evoke some of the strongest memories of their lives. More than 40 years after the end of the war, cartoonists still referred to its events.

"Their Tearjerker"
by Joseph Parrish, appeared in the *Chicago Tribune*, 1946
Harry S. Truman Library, National Archives

"The Shape Of Things Now"
by Daniel Robert Fitzpatrick, appeared in the *St. Louis Post-Dispatch*, March 4, 1945
Victoria Schuck Collection at the John Fitzgerald Kennedy Library, National Archives
Fitzpatrick in the *St. Louis Post-Dispatch*

POST–WORLD WAR II

Americans joyfully celebrated the end of World War II. While the United States emerged from the war with a booming economy, much of Europe was ravaged, war torn, and starving. The United States provided food and other forms of aid to help revitalize and stabilize the economies of European countries.

LIBERATED EUROPE
MAR. 4. 45
THE SHAPE OF THINGS NOW.
ST. LOUIS POST-DISPATCH

"Hands Across The Sea"
by [illegible], probably appeared in the *San Francisco News*, Scripps-Howard News Service, not dated
Harry S. Truman Library, National Archives

"Down to Bottomless Perdition"
by Daniel Robert Fitzpatrick, appeared in the *St. Louis Post-Dispatch*, May 7, 1945
Victoria Schuck Collection at the John Fitzgerald Kennedy Library, National Archives
Fitzpatrick in the *St. Louis Post-Dispatch*

"I Wear It Where I Need It."
by Bill Mauldin, appeared in the *Chicago Sun-Times*, May 21, 1965
Lyndon Baines Johnson Library, National Archives
Reprinted with permission of Bill Mauldin

". . . Meanwhile Back on the Home Front"
by Gene Basset, Scripps-Howard News Service, November 1, 1965
Lyndon Baines Johnson Library, National Archives
Reprinted through the courtesy of Gene Basset and Scripps-Howard News Service

VIETNAM WAR

In contrast to World War II, the war in Vietnam did not enjoy the full support of the American people. The cartoons of the 1960s and 1970s reflect a divided homefront. The war issue pitted different generations and different segments of society against one another. American leadership was besieged by dissent.

...MEANWHILE BACK ON THE HOME FRONT

TO LYNDON JOHNSON, WITH BEST WISHES — GENE BASSET

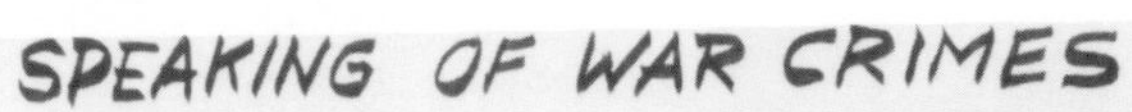
SPEAKING OF WAR CRIMES

VIET CONG
GENEVA CONVENTION
Ed Valtman '65
The Hartford Times

"How Deep You Figure We'll Get Involved, Sir!"
by Bil Canfield, appeared in the *Newark* (NJ) *Star-Ledger*, not dated
National Press Club Collection, Washington, DC
Reprinted through the courtesy of Bil Canfield and the *Newark* (NJ) *Star-Ledger*

"Speaking of War Crimes"
by Edmund Valtman, appeared in the *Hartford Times*, October 2, 1965
Lyndon Baines Johnson Library, National Archives
Reprinted through the courtesy of Edmund Valtman and the *Hartford Times*

[LBJ and Vietnam Specters]
by J. Paul Szep, appeared in the *Boston Globe*, 1960s
Library of Congress, Prints and Photographs Division
Reprinted through the courtesy of Paul Szep and the *Boston Globe*

"He Was Talking about Vietnam and Then—"
by Bruce Shanks, appeared in the *Buffalo Evening News*, April 1, 1968
Lyndon Baines Johnson Library, National Archives
Reprinted through the courtesy of the *Buffalo Evening News*

"There's a War On?"
by Warren King, appeared in the *New York Daily News*, 1966
Lyndon Baines Johnson Library, National Archives
© 1966 New York News, Inc., reprinted with permission

In the face of growing criticism over American involvement in the war, President Lyndon B. Johnson in 1966 maintained that the United States could remain involved in Vietnam without sacrificing any of the social programs known collectively as "The Great Society."

"Pick Up Your Checks At The Rear Door. This Entrance Is For Real Veterans."
by Oliphant, appeared in the *Denver Post*, April 24, 1974
Reprinted through the courtesy of the Susan Conway Carroll Gallery, Washington, DC

POST–VIETNAM WAR

The legacy of the bitter domestic conflict over the Vietnam war is eloquently expressed in these cartoons

"Chill In The Room"
by Bert Whitman, appeared in the *Phoenix Gazette*, January 7, 1977
Jimmy Carter Library, National Archives
Used with permission. Permission does not imply endorsement.

On January 21, 1977, President Carter issued a pardon for most of those who had resisted the draft during the Vietnam war years.

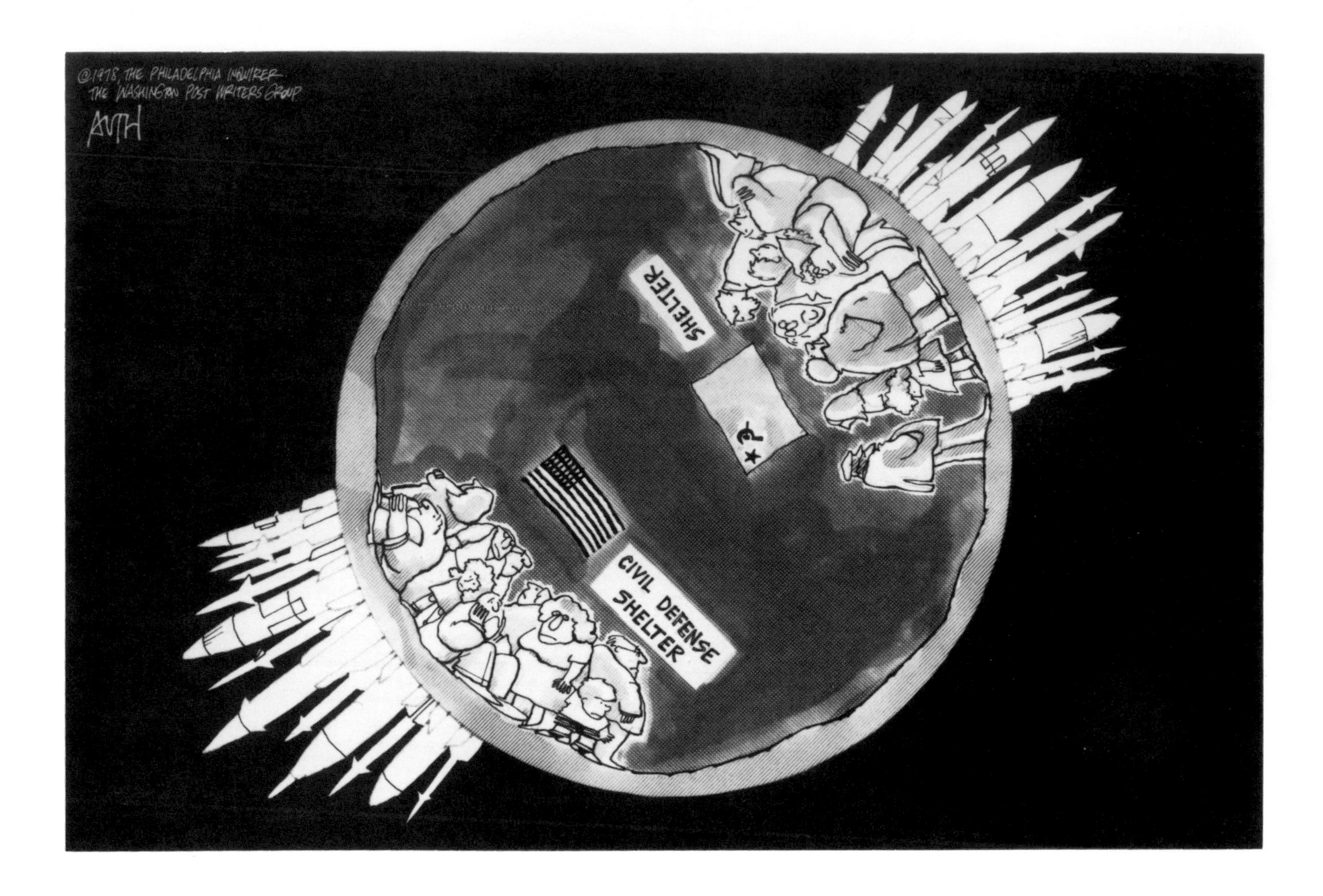

[Long-Distance View of the Arms Race]
by Tony Auth, appeared in the *Philadelphia Inquirer*, November 15, 1978
National Press Club Collection, Washington, DC
Reprinted through the courtesy of Tony Auth and the *Philadelphia Inquirer*

"Hiroshima"
by Robert Osborn, 1945
Library of Congress, Prints and Photographs Division
Reprinted through the courtesy of Robert Osborn

THE NUCLEAR ERA

The two atomic bombs dropped on Japan in 1945 ushered in the age of nuclear warfare. The threat of nuclear weapons looms over the conduct of foreign affairs to this day.

Osborn

POLITICAL CORRUPTION

The American people respond with both outrage and disappointment to reports of political corruption. As political commentators, cartoonists are swift to express the outrage engendered by any betrayal of the public trust. Their work reaffirms the conviction that, in this country, no individual is above the law.

"Washington Bomb"
by Daniel Robert Fitzpatrick, appeared in the *St. Louis Post-Dispatch*, January 1942
Harry S. Truman Library, National Archives
Fitzpatrick in the *St. Louis Post-Dispatch*

Senator Harry S. Truman rose to national prominence in the early 1940s because of his exposure of corruption within the national defense contracting system. He headed a Senate investigative committee whose revelations are reported to have saved the nation some $15 billion.

WASHINGTON BOMB.

"The Tammany Tiger Loose, What Are You Going To Do About It?"
by Thomas Nast, appeared in *Harper's Weekly*, November 11, 1871
Office of Public Programs, National Archives

Here, the tiger, which has wreaked havoc on the "Republic," "the law," "the ballot box," and "power," is a symbol for the corrupt Democratic Party. "Boss" Tweed appears in the background, brandishing the victor's "iron rod."

Thomas Nast (1840–1902) is often described as the father of the American political cartoon. Although cartoons had existed in America since colonial times, few had the political impact of Nast's drawings.

"Who Stole the People's Money? Do Tell. 'Twas Him"
by Thomas Nast, appeared in *Harper's Weekly*,
August 17, 1871
Office of Public Programs, National Archives

The Tammany Ring, headed by William Marcy ("Boss") Tweed, is known to have swindled millions of dollars from the people of New York City. This cartoon shows the Tammany Ring in a classic "pass-the-buck" pose. Tweed is the fat, bearded figure on the left.

His most famous body of work, published in *Harper's Weekly* from 1869 to 1871, targeted the corruption within the New York City Democratic Party's political machine, which was known as Tammany Hall. Through a series of some 50 hard-hitting drawings, Nast aimed at nothing short of bringing the guilty culprits to justice.

"Can the Law Reach Him?"
by Thomas Nast, appeared in *Harper's Weekly*, January 6, 1872
Office of Public Programs, National Archives

"If This Thing Grows Much Bigger I May Have To Drop It"
by John C. Conacher, 1924
Library of Congress, Prints and Photographs Division

The Teapot Dome scandal came to symbolize the many incidents of corruption that infected the Harding administration (1921–23). Government-owned oil reserves in Teapot Dome, WY, and Elk Hills, CA, were secretly and illegally leased by Secretary of the Interior Albert Fall to private oil companies. "Teapot Dome" became a catch phrase for the incidents of corruption that were discovered in several government agencies.

OIL SCANDALS

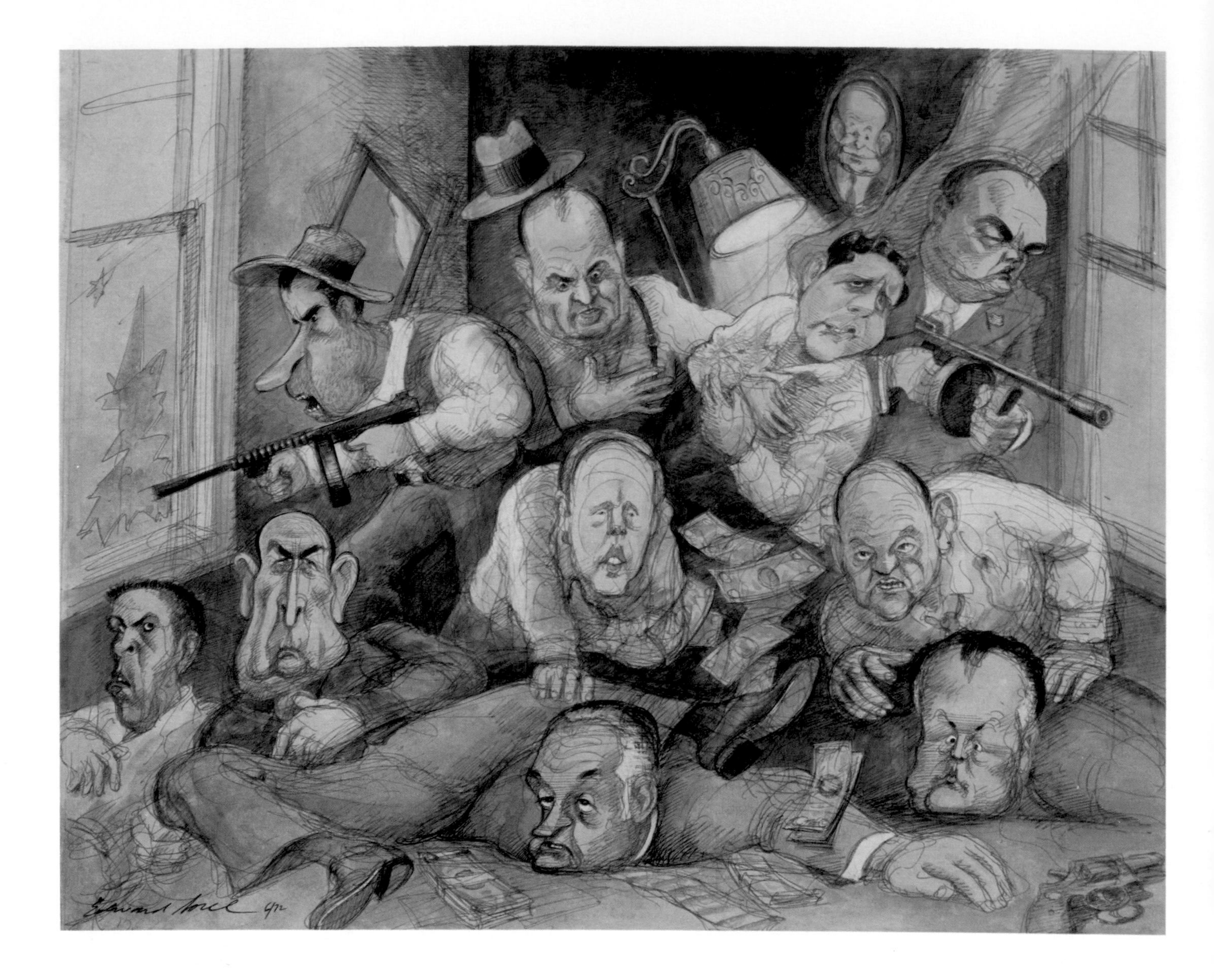

The Watergate affair, named for the site of the 1972 break-in of the Democratic National Committee headquarters, dominated the Presidency of Richard Nixon throughout 1973 and continued until he resigned in August 1974. The public was shocked to learn of the extent of espionage and other abuses. As more and more members of the White House staff were implicated in the affair, President Nixon continued to deny knowledge of the break-in or the subsequent cover-up.

"Watergate Shoot-Out"
by Edward Sorel, appeared in *Ramparts*, June 1972
Collection of Byron Dobell
Reprinted through the courtesy of Edward Sorel

Casualties of the "Watergate Shoot-Out" include the following high-ranking government officials and White House advisers: President Richard Nixon, Jeb Magruder and Jim McCord of the Citizens Committee for the Reelection of the President (CREEP), John Ehrlichman, Patrick Gray, Richard Kleindienst, Maurice Stans, John Dean, John Mitchell, and H. R. Haldeman.

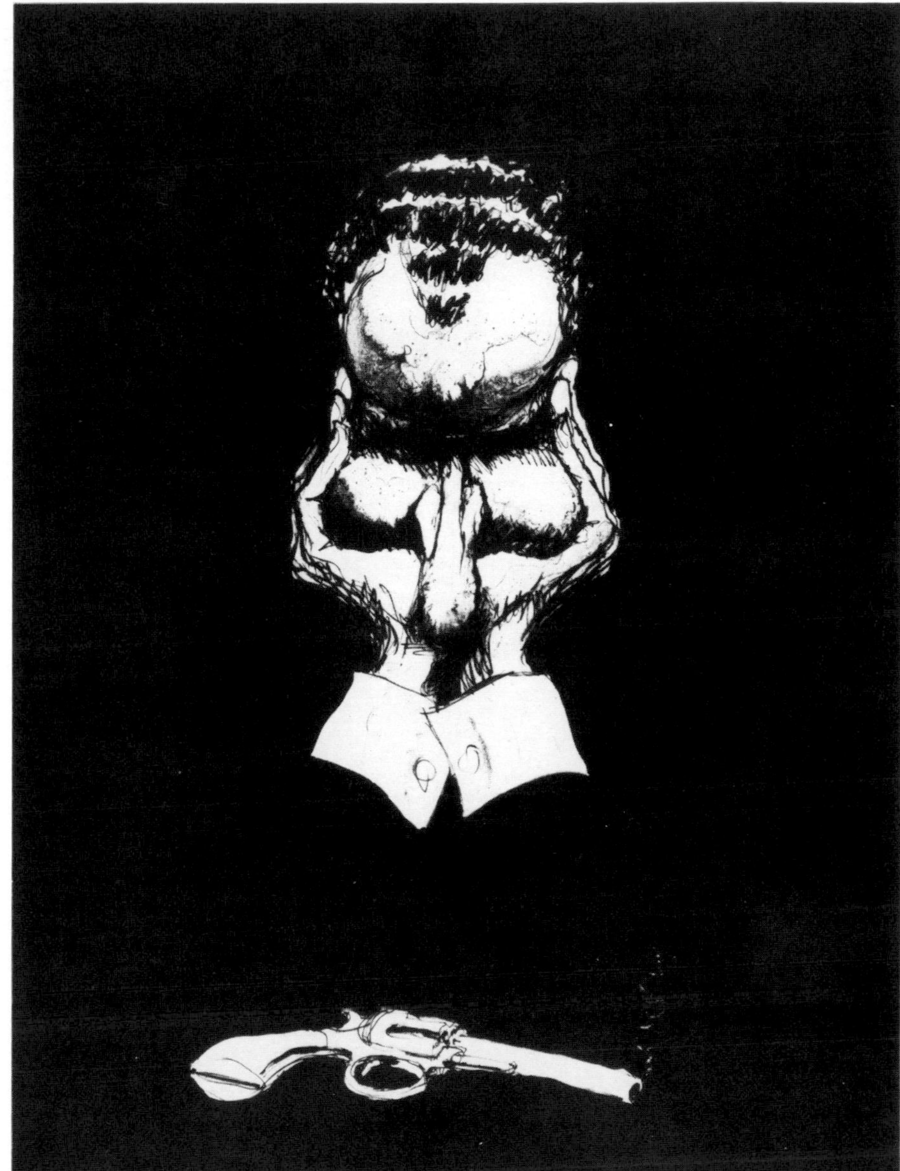

"The Smoking Gun"
by Oliphant, 1984
Reprinted through the courtesy of the Susan Conway Carroll Gallery, Washington, DC

The "smoking gun" of the Watergate scandal referred to a tape recording of a White House conversation revealing that soon after the Watergate break-in, President Nixon impeded an FBI investigation of the incident and ordered his aides to participate in a cover-up.

'I HAVE DISCOVERED THAT ACCORDING TO A SECRET TAPE OF JUNE 23, 1972, I AM A CROOK.'

"I Have Discovered That According To a Secret Tape of June 23, 1972, I *Am* a Crook."
by Bill Sanders, appeared in the *Milwaukee Journal*, August 6, 1974
National Press Club Collection, Washington, DC
Reprinted through the courtesy of Bill Sanders

"Really! Spiro!"
by Lou Grant, appeared in the *Oakland Tribune*, 1973
Collection of Lou Grant
Reprinted through the courtesy of Lou Grant and the *Oakland Tribune*

In August 1973 Vice President Agnew revealed that he was under investigation by the Justice Department in connection with official corruption in the Maryland state government that took place while Agnew served as Governor. Although he denied all charges of wrongdoing, Agnew resigned the office of Vice President on October 10; he pleaded no contest to one charge of income tax evasion in return for the dropping of other charges.

"Just Let Me Leave With My Dignity Intact"
by Ed Stein, appeared in the *Rocky Mountain News*, Newspaper Enterprise Alliance, 1989
Collection of Ed Stein
Reprinted through the courtesy of Ed Stein

In 1989 Speaker of the House Jim Wright ended a distinguished career amid allegations of wrongdoing.

"As A Matter Of Fact I *Do* Work for H.U.D. . . . Why Do You Ask? . ."
by Walt Handelsman, appeared in the *Scranton Times*, 1989
Collection of Walt Handelsman
Reprinted through the courtesy of Walt Handelsman and the *Scranton Times*

In 1989 financial scandals within the Department of Housing and Urban Development (HUD) came to light. Public funds intended for middle-income home-owners and the poor were alleged to have been diverted to wealthy real estate developers.

PRESIDENTIAL CARICATURES

The President is a powerful living symbol of government. With heightened expectations, the American people have come to hold the President responsible for everything that is right or wrong with the government at a particular time.

Political cartoonists often seize on public perceptions that already exist. By selecting a single personal characteristic of the President — a smile, a gesture, a hairstyle — the successful cartoonist can create a single image that speaks volumes about what kind of job we think our government is doing.

"George Bush"
by Oliphant
Bronze, 1989
Courtesy of the Susan Conway Carroll Gallery, Washington, DC

HOW WILL HOOVER GO DOWN IN HISTORY.
WE KNOW HOW HE LOOKED WHEN HE WAS ELECTED_ BUT–?
THE BRAINY IDEALIST ?
OR THE HARD BOILED EXECUTIVE ?
THE ARDENT DRY ?
THE COMMONER OR THE ARISTOCRAT ?
AS EUROPE CHARICATURES HIM?
THE GREAT THINKER?
OR THE GREAT DOER ?
THE FALSE ALARM ?
SWEETENED BY ADVERSITY OR SOURED BY DISILLUSIONMENT

HERBERT HOOVER

In October 1929, 7 months after Herbert Hoover became President, the stock market crash marked the beginning of the Great Depression. Hoover believed that direct federal payments to the poor and hungry would undermine individual initiative and private charity. Although he was deeply distressed by his country's suffering, he failed to communicate his concern, and his measures proved to be inadequate.

By the time he left office on March 4, 1933, the man whose name was once associated with humanitarianism soon became synonymous with the Depression's most painful aspects.

"How Will Hoover Go Down in History?"
by Jay Norwood "Ding" Darling, appeared in the *Des Moines Register and Leader*, August 26, 1929
Herbert Hoover Library, National Archives

FRANKLIN D. ROOSEVELT

By the time Franklin D. Roosevelt became President in 1933, the Great Depression had dominated American life for more than 3 years. Once in office, he aggressively fought the effects of the Depression with a flurry of government programs that aimed at bringing relief to the economy and to the common man.

Roosevelt's bold style of leadership struck a chord in the hearts of the American people. While his ardent supporters found his confidence, energy, and vigor reassuring, his critics viewed those same traits as arrogant. His strong personality and distinctive personal style made him a popular subject for cartoonists.

[Caricature of Franklin D. Roosevelt]
by Eugene Alenquist, not dated
Franklin D. Roosevelt Library, National Archives

The wide smile, the prominent chin, and the pince-nez are often featured in cartoon portrayals of President Roosevelt.

HARRY S. TRUMAN

Harry S. Truman became President of the United States on April 12, 1945, upon the death of President Roosevelt. Although Truman had earned a reputation for honesty and efficiency, he seemed to the American people to be both uneasy and inexperienced.

He won over many of the American people with his genuine concern for the common person and no-nonsense approach to government business. His adopted slogan, "the buck stops here," reflected his willingness to make difficult decisions and stick by them.

Cartoonists often portrayed Truman as the feisty "everyman" — the underdog from the heartland of America who fought hard for the causes of the people.

[Caricature of Harry S. Truman]
by Otto Soglow, October 3, 1949
Harry S. Truman Library, National Archives
Reprinted through the courtesy of King Features Syndicate, Inc.

"Time Flies — And So Does Harry"
by Cy Hungerford, appeared in the *Pittsburgh Post-Gazette*, April 1950
Harry S. Truman Library, National Archives
Reprinted through the courtesy of Cy Hungerford and the *Pittsburgh Post-Gazette*

Truman succeeded one of the most beloved Presidents in American history. Accustomed to Roosevelt's strong leadership, the American people thought Truman incapable of filling Roosevelt's shoes. Eventually, Truman's strong and decisive style of leadership surprised many Americans.

O. SOGLOW

INFECTIOUS

DWIGHT D. EISENHOWER

Having led the Allied Forces in Europe to victory in World War II, Dwight D. Eisenhower was one of the most popular men in postwar America. He was elected President in 1952 by a landslide.

The period of Eisenhower's Presidency, the years of "Peace and Prosperity," is also called the "Age of Suspicion." The years that saw a robust economy and the birth of the space program and the interstate highway system are also the years of the cold war abroad and an anticommunist fever at home. Racial tension and violence increased following the 1954 Supreme Court decision outlawing segregation of public schools.

Eisenhower presided over these times. Although many people criticized his centrist approach to politics, many others found his unpretentious charm and low-key personality appealing. Cartoonists often portrayed him with affection. His famous smile was often described as "infectious."

"Infectious"
by Joseph Parrish, appeared in the *Chicago Tribune*, 1955
Dwight D. Eisenhower Library, National Archives

JOHN F. KENNEDY

When John F. Kennedy ran for President in 1960, he was 43 years old. As the youngest man ever to be elected President, he had to dispel the image of an untried, immature man with little experience. Eventually his youth, energy, and glamor endeared him to many of the American people.

Once elected, he challenged the American people to join him in a quest for the "New Frontier." He called upon the people to choose public service over private pursuits — to choose progress over normalcy during the prosperous postwar years.

"The New Look"
by Art Wood, appeared in the *Pittsburgh Press*, February 8, 1960
John Fitzgerald Kennedy Library, National Archives
Reprinted with permission of the *Pittsburgh Press*

THE NEW LOOK
YESTERDAY
THE KENNEDY WAVE
TODAY

LYNDON B. JOHNSON

President Johnson was a natural politician. He wheedled, cajoled, armtwisted, and bulldozed members of Congress to pass his social programs known collectively as "The Great Society." In spite of major achievements in the areas of civil rights and social reform, Johnson's Presidency was overshadowed by the growing unpopularity of the war in Vietnam.

President Johnson was a popular subject for cartoonists. Many of them focused on Johnson's unbridled enthusiasm for the game of politics, his Texas roots, and his considerable gifts as a persuader. A common theme was the schizophrenic nature of the Johnson Presidency: the popular domestic policies — war on poverty, disease, and injustice — in contrast with the unpopular involvement in the Vietnam war.

[LBJ] Showing His Scar, Shaped Like A Map Of Vietnam]
by David Levine, appeared in the *New York Review of Books*, 1966
Lyndon Baines Johnson Library, National Archives
Drawing by David Levine. Reprinted with permission from *The New York Review of Books*. Copyright © 1966–1981 Nyrev, Inc.

While recuperating from gall bladder surgery in 1965, President Johnson showed off his new scar to a group of reporters and photographers. Millions of Americans shared in the moment when a photograph of the gesture appeared in *Life* magazine. In David Levine's caricature, the exposed scar takes on the shape of a map of Vietnam.

[LBJ] and Two Cherubs: Domestic Policy, Foreign Policy]
by Bob Taylor, appeared in the *Dallas Times-Herald*, January 13, 1965
Lyndon Baines Johnson Library, National Archives
Reprinted through the courtesy of the *Dallas Times-Herald*

For the collection of the
Lyndon Baines Johnson Library
& Museum

RICHARD M. NIXON

Richard M. Nixon served as President from January 1969 to August 1974. The Nixon administration made major breakthroughs in the area of foreign affairs, including the initiation of arms limitation talks with the Soviet Union, the renewal of relations with the People's Republic of China, and the end of American involvement in Southeast Asia. Nevertheless, Nixon's tenure as President remains inextricably linked to the political scandal known as Watergate.

[Caricature of President Nixon in Prison Stripes Chained to the "Press"]
by Jeff MacNelly, appeared in the *Richmond News Leader*, not dated
National Press Club Collection, Washington, DC
Reprinted through the courtesy of Jeff MacNelly

MACNELLY THE RICHMOND NEWS LEADER
To the NATIONAL PRESS CLUB —
PRESS

GENTLEMEN, WE'RE SUPPOSED TO BE PROTECTING OUR CHIEF
BRUISED IN FLORIDA SWIMMING POOL
BUMPED BY CHILD WITH FLAG STAFF
TRIPPED OVER WOMAN IN WHEEL CHAIR
OLD FOOTBALL INJURY
HAIL TO THE CHIEF
SECRET SERVICE
ROBERTS
11/10/75

GERALD R. FORD

Gerald Ford assumed the Presidency on August 9, 1974, when Richard Nixon resigned. Ford's reputation for honesty, respectability, and good-naturedness restored public confidence in the White House. President Ford's pardon of Richard Nixon for any crimes he had committed or may have committed as President cost Ford a great deal of public support.

Cartoonists had a field day with a series of Ford's missteps and stumbles. In many cartoons, these incidents became a metaphor for Ford's overall competence to serve.

"Gentlemen, We're Supposed To Be Protecting Our Chief"
by Bill Roberts, appeared in the *Cleveland Press*,
Scripps-Howard News Service, November 10, 1975
Gerald R. Ford Museum, National Archives
Reprinted through the courtesy of Mrs. William E. Roberts

JIMMY CARTER

Jimmy Carter was elected President in 1976. During the campaign, he emphasized his moral values as a born-again Christian, his naval career, his tenure as Governor of Georgia, and his success as a peanut farmer.

Once elected, his aversion to the Washington political scene worked against him. Members of Congress opposed his programs, and the press corps perceived him as aloof. He was often portrayed as lacking the sophistication and leadership ability necessary to meet the demands of the office.

[Peanut Caricature of Jimmy Carter]
by Tom Curtis, appeared in the *Milwaukee Sentinel*, January 20, 1977
Jimmy Carter Library, National Archives
Reprinted through the courtesy of the *Milwaukee Sentinel*

"'Well, I'll Be A Fiddle Stompin', Goose Hollerin' Son Of A Gun. . . . Lookie Thar, Jimmy! There's Old Fred Stumps From Plains. . . . Hey . . . Come On Up Here, Fred, And Have A Beer . . .!'"
by Ed Gamble, appeared in the *Nashville Banner*, 1977
Jimmy Carter Library, National Archives
Reprinted through the courtesy of Ed Gamble and the *Nashville Banner*

"WELL, I'LL BE A FIDDLE STOMPIN', goose hollerin' son OF A gun... LOOKIE THAR, JIMMY! THERE'S OLD FRED STUMPS FROM PLAINS... HEY... COME ON UP here, FRED, AND HAVE A BEER...!"

RONALD REAGAN

Ronald Reagan was elected President in 1980, overwhelmingly defeating Jimmy Carter. To heal the nation's weakening economy, Reagan proposed deep cuts in the federal budget and tax cuts. In spite of Presidential assurances that there would be a "safety net" to protect the truly needy, many remained skeptical.

"Sir . . . Do You Think You're Too Old To Run? . . . Sure My Old Movies Were Fun . . ."
by Mike Peters, appeared in the *Dayton Daily News*, 1984
Collection of Mike Peters
Reprinted through the courtesy of Mike Peters, *Dayton Daily News*

Ronald Reagan was 70 years old when he became President. Throughout his Presidency, cartoonists lampooned him for his earlier career as a Hollywood actor as well as for his advanced age.

"Let 'em eat cake"
by David Levine, 1981
Library of Congress, Prints and Photographs Division
Drawing by David Levine. Reprinted with permission from *The New York Review of Books*. Copyright © 1966-1981 Nyrev, Inc.

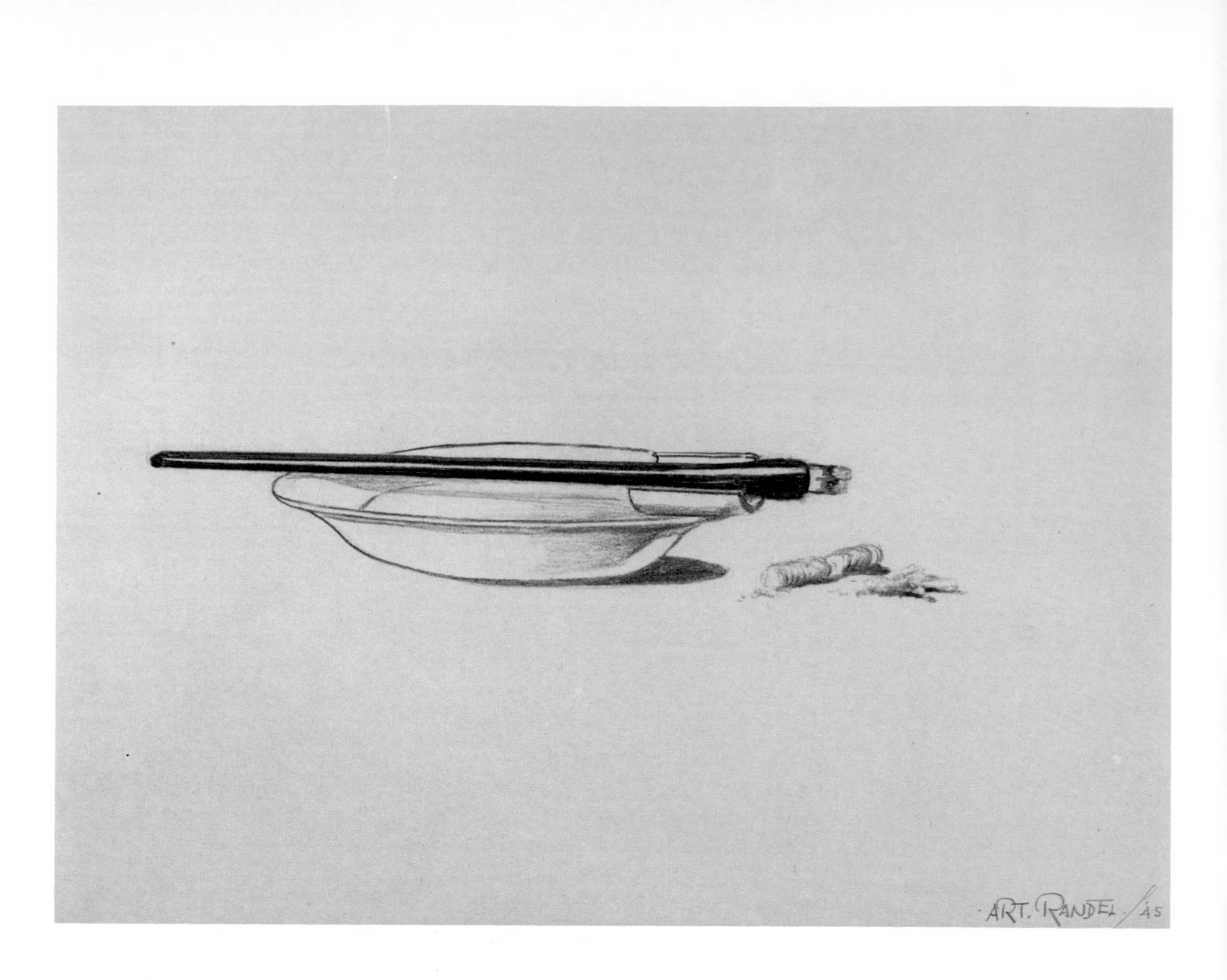

POST-MORTEM TRIBUTES

[President Franklin D. Roosevelt's Cigarette Holder]
by Art Randel, 1945
Franklin D. Roosevelt Library, National Archives

[Lincoln Mourning the Death of President Kennedy]
by Bill Mauldin, appeared in the *Chicago Sun-Times*, November 22, 1963
John Fitzgerald Kennedy Library, National Archives
Reprinted with permission of Bill Mauldin

President Kennedy was assassinated on November 22, 1963, provoking an outpouring of grief throughout the world. This cartoon was drawn, printed, and distributed within hours of the assassination.

For Mrs. Jacqueline Kennedy
©1963 MAULDIN
Chicago Sun-Times

"See What You Can Do About Digging Up a Piano . . ."
by Oliphant, appeared in the *Denver Post*,
1972
Harry S. Truman Library, National Archives
Reprinted through the courtesy of the Susan Conway Carroll Gallery, Washington, DC

Published upon Truman's death in 1972, this cartoon refers to Truman's hobby of playing the piano, as it pokes fun at his forthrightness.

[Horse Without A Rider]
by Paul Conrad, appeared in the *Los Angeles Times*,
January 1973
Lyndon Baines Johnson Library, National Archives
Copyright, 1973, Los Angeles Times. Reprinted with permission

This riderless horse, a classic symbol of a fallen warrior, appeared upon the death of President Johnson in 1973.

LBJ
1973, The Register
and Tribune Syndicate
CONRAD
©.THE LOS ANGELES TIMES, 1973

RACE FOR THE WHITE HOUSE

Every 4 years, we engage in one of our favorite national pastimes: the Presidential election. The road to a Presidential election is a complicated route of caucuses, primaries, and conventions. The system that provides for a peaceful and orderly transfer of executive power is full of drama and suspense.

Modern cartoonists delight in portraying the political posturing, competition, color, and vitality of this unique American institution.

[Franklin D. Roosevelt and Herbert Hoover]
by Peter Arno, cover of the *New Yorker*, March 4, 1933
Franklin D. Roosevelt Library, National Archives

This magazine cover shows a jubilant Franklin Roosevelt and a morose Herbert Hoover on their way to Roosevelt's first inauguration. It was never published, due to the February 15, 1933, attempt to assassinate Roosevelt, in which Chicago's Mayor Anton Čermak was fatally wounded.

Mar. 4, 1933
THE
NEW YORKER
Price 15 cents
Peter
Arno

3RD TERM QUESTION
FARLEY
GARNER
McNUTT
WHEELER
LEO JOSEPH ROCHE

"The Sphinx — 1940 Model"
by Leo Joseph Roche, appeared in the *Buffalo Courier Express*, November 16, 1939
Franklin D. Roosevelt Library, National Archives

In 1939 President Franklin Roosevelt was portrayed as the sphinx, while the public wondered whether or not he would choose to run for an unprecedented third term. His advisers Farley, Garner, McNutt, and Wheeler are also shown.

"I Want Y'All"
by Blaine, appeared in the *Hamilton Spectator* (Ontario, Canada), 1964
Lyndon Baines Johnson Library, National Archives
Reprinted through the courtesy of Blaine, the *Hamilton Spectator*, Canada

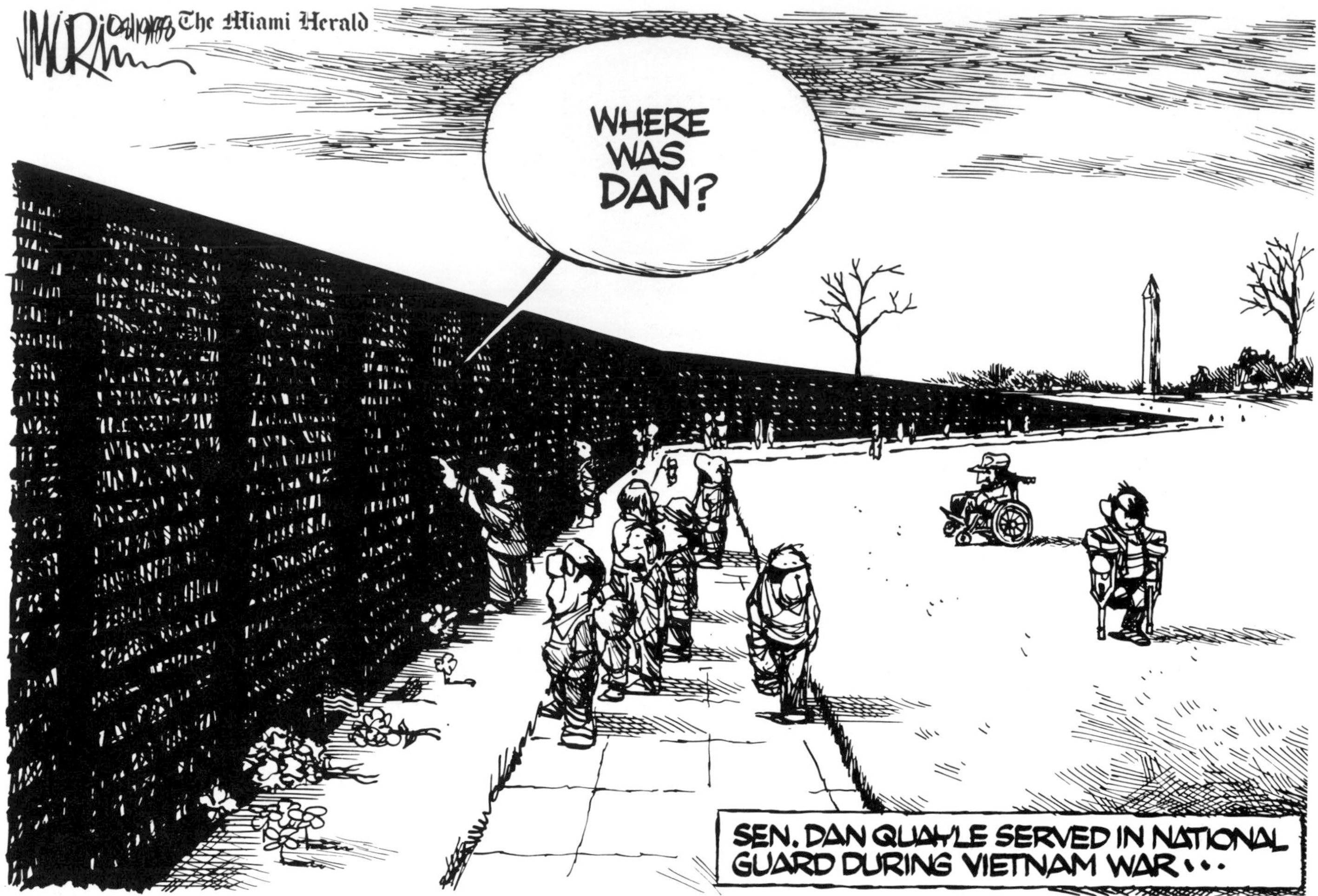

"Where Was Dan?"
by Jim Morin, appeared in the *Miami Herald*, August 19, 1988
Collection of Jim Morin
Reprinted through the courtesy of Jim Morin and the *Miami Herald*

"Two Responses to Country's Call"
by Thomas Nast, 1892
Franklin D. Roosevelt Library, National Archives

It is common for political opponents to point out each other's shortcomings. During the elections of 1892 and 1988, Presidential candidate Grover Cleveland and Vice-Presidential candidate Dan Quayle were portrayed as avoiding the fulfillment of their military obligations.

LITTLE BEN. "COME ON BOYS! WE'VE NEVER BEEN LICKED YET, AND WE WON'T BEGIN NOW!"
17th INDIANA REGIMENT U.S.V.
U.S.
TWO RESPONSES TO THE COUNTRY'S CALL.
OH! MY PRECIOUS SELF!
U.S.
YOU G. CLEVELA
DRAFTED IN THE U.S SERVICE.
A. LINCOLN
"MY COUNTRY AND MY FLAG!"
HARRISON.
Th: Nast. 1892.
"HOW MUCH FOR A SUBSTITUTE?"
CLEVELAND

NO PLACE FOR A KIDDIE CAR.

"Hi — My Name's Jimmy Carter — I Told You So!"
by Bill Garner, appeared in the *Commercial Appeal*, 1977
Jimmy Carter Library, National Archives
Reprinted through the courtesy of Bill Garner and the *Commercial Appeal*

"No Place for a Kiddie Car"
by Daniel Robert Fitzpatrick, appeared in the *St. Louis Post-Dispatch*, March 29, 1940
Harry S. Truman Library, National Archives
Fitzpatrick in the *St. Louis Post-Dispatch*

The underdog winner holds a special place in the hearts of Americans. This image of Harry S. Truman as a "Kiddie Car" in the 1940 senatorial primary in Missouri proved to be a harbinger of the 1948 Presidential election — one of America's greatest upset victories, in which Truman defeated Thomas Dewey.

BALANCE OF POWER

The U.S. Constitution distributes federal power among three branches of government. An elaborate system of checks and balances keeps the executive, legislative, and judicial branches in a perpetual state of tension with each other.

These drawings show the President, the Congress, and the Supreme Court in an uneasy equilibrium.

"The Balance of Power"
by Burris Jenkins, Jr., appeared in the *New York World Telegram*, April 1952
Harry S. Truman Library, National Archives

During the Korean war, when a shutdown of the American steel industry seemed inevitable due to a labor dispute, President Truman seized the mills. Two months later, the Supreme Court ruled that the seizure was unconstitutional, confirming the charges that the President had overstepped his executive authority.

THE BALANCE OF POWER!

"Another Boundary Dispute!"
by Walter J. Enright, appeared in the *Evening World*, ca. 1929–30
Herbert Hoover Library, National Archives

"And When Did You First Notice We Weren't Listening?"
by Hy Rosen, appeared in the *Albany Times Union*, April 13, 1975
Gerald R. Ford Museum, National Archives
Reprinted through the courtesy of Hy Rosen

President Ford's request for military aid to Saigon in 1975 fell on deaf congressional ears.

"Frankly, Scarletface — Ah don't give dams . . ."
by Corky Trinidad, appeared in the *Honolulu Star-Bulletin*, 1977
Jimmy Carter Library, National Archives
Reprinted through the courtesy of Corky Trinidad, *Honolulu Star-Bulletin*

"A Presidential Touch"
by Cy Hungerford, appeared in the *Pittsburgh Post-Gazette*, January 17, 1957
Dwight D. Eisenhower Library, National Archives
Reprinted through the courtesy of Cy Hungerford and the *Pittsburgh Post-Gazette*

A PRESIDENTIAL TOUCH.
BROTHER-
CAN YOU SPARE
ABOUT 72 BILLION
DOLLARS
?
IKE
CONGRESS
Good Luck to Ike from Cy Hungerford Pgh Post-Gazette Jan 17 1957
HUNGERFORD

THE LIGHTNING SPEED OF HONESTY.

THE GALLOPING SNAIL

"The Lightning Speed of Honesty"
by Thomas Nast, appeared in *Harper's Weekly*, November 24, 1877
Office of Public Programs, National Archives

In this illustration Uncle Sam, with military budget in hand, rides Congress, symbolized by a snail. This is one of many cartoons in which Nast criticized low peacetime military budgets.

"The Galloping Snail"
by Burt Thomas, appeared in the *Detroit News*, ca. March 20, 1933
Franklin D. Roosevelt Library, National Archives
Reprinted through the courtesy of the *Detroit News*

President Franklin D. Roosevelt, New Deal legislation in hand, is shown riding Congress, which is symbolized, again, by a snail. The cartoon refers to the flurry of legislation enacted in the beginning of Roosevelt's first administration, known as the "100 Days," to provide relief and recovery from the Great Depression.

These two drawings, drawn 56 years apart, use the same snail images to depict a classic American political reality — that one branch of government restrains another.

"New Deal Plan for Enlarged Supreme Court"
by Clifford K. Berryman, appeared in the *Washington Evening Star*, February 10, 1937
Library of Congress, Prints and Photographs Division

In 1937 President Roosevelt proposed a plan to enlarge the Supreme Court. Such a plan would enable him to appoint justices who would be more sympathetic to the President's programs. Neither Congress nor the public would accept any tampering with the Supreme Court. This plan, which came to be known as an attempt to "pack the Court," was defeated in Congress.

Harold Ickes, Secretary of the Interior and head of the Public Works Administration (PWA), appears shocked to learn of Roosevelt's plan to enlarge the Court.

"Modern Crucifixion — by the Nine Ancients — 1935 A.D."
by Harry S. Outhwaite, 1935
Franklin D. Roosevelt Library, National Archives

The New Deal programs that fought the effects of the Great Depression expanded federal power. In 1935 and 1936 the Supreme Court struck down several New Deal laws for being unconstitutional — for overreaching the limits of constitutional authority.

President Roosevelt and many of his supporters believed that the Court was holding back the country's progress in fighting the Depression. This drawing shows the nine Supreme Court justices, "nine ancients," surrounding three crucified pieces of the New Deal plan, including the National Recovery Administration (NRA).

THE EXECUTIVE AND THE JUDICIARY

MODERN CRUCIFIXION - BY THE NINE ANCIENTS. - 1935 A.D.

"History's Burlesque"
by Joseph Parrish, appeared in the *Chicago Tribune*, 1949
Harry S. Truman Library, National Archives

Harry S. Truman vetoed the Taft-Hartley bill, which limited the powers of organized labor. The law was enacted over his veto in 1947. In 1949 President Truman called on Congress to repeal the measure, which he had described as a "slave labor law." This cartoon reflects the fear that Truman might overstep his authority in pursuit of his policies.

"Milhous I"
by Edward Sorel, appeared in *Rolling Stone*, March 14, 1974
Library of Congress, Prints and Photographs Division
Reprinted through the courtesy of Edward Sorel

San Clemente, CA, and Key Biscayne, FL, were the sites of two of Nixon's homes.

"King George IV"
by Paul Conrad, appeared in the *Los Angeles Times*, December 1990
Collection of Paul Conrad

Following President Bush's decision to increase the number of U.S. forces in the Persian Gulf, Conrad merged the identities of King George III of England and George Bush to create King George IV.

IMPERIAL PRESIDENCY

The United States was born in 1776 in a revolt against a king. The trappings of royalty have come to symbolize the excesses of executive power. Cartoonists recall 18th-century monarchs as the ultimate symbol of government excess and abuse of power.

MILHOUS I
Lord of San Clemente
Duke of Key Biscayne
Captain of Watergate
Edward Sorel '74

— WHITE HOUSE SOLITAIRE —

[Doonesbury Strip — "Jerry, I've Been Meaning to Talk to You for Some Time"]
by Garry Trudeau, Universal Press Syndicate, June 24, 1974
Gerald R. Ford Museum, National Archives
Reprinted through the courtesy of Garry Trudeau

In June 1974 Garry Trudeau created this imaginary dialogue between Vice President Ford and President Nixon. In the conversation Nixon referred to his press secretary, Ron Ziegler, who was replaced when Gerald Ford became President.

"White House Solitaire"
by Franklin O. Alexander, appeared in the *Philadelphia Evening Bulletin*, September 23, 1966
Lyndon Baines Johnson Library, National Archives
Reprinted through the courtesy of Franklin O. Alexander

Nicholas Katzenbach served as Attorney General from 1961 until 1966, when President Johnson appointed him Under Secretary of State.

THE DRAMA OF EXECUTIVE STAFFING

As head of the executive branch of government, the President oversees the work of more than 3 million federal workers. The Constitution allows him to hire, with the consent of Congress, or fire the highest ranking officers in the executive branch.

DOMESTIC ISSUES

The notion of individual liberties is one of the most treasured principles of American government. But personal freedom is not absolute. Citizens of the United States give up a measure of freedom in exchange for security.

The degree to which Americans are subject to restrictions on their liberty has always been subject to debate. In the face of a national crisis such as war, civil unrest, or economic catastrophe, Americans may tolerate greater government involvement in their lives. Like most issues of common concern, such debates are aired in the cartoons and articles on the editorial pages of our newspapers.

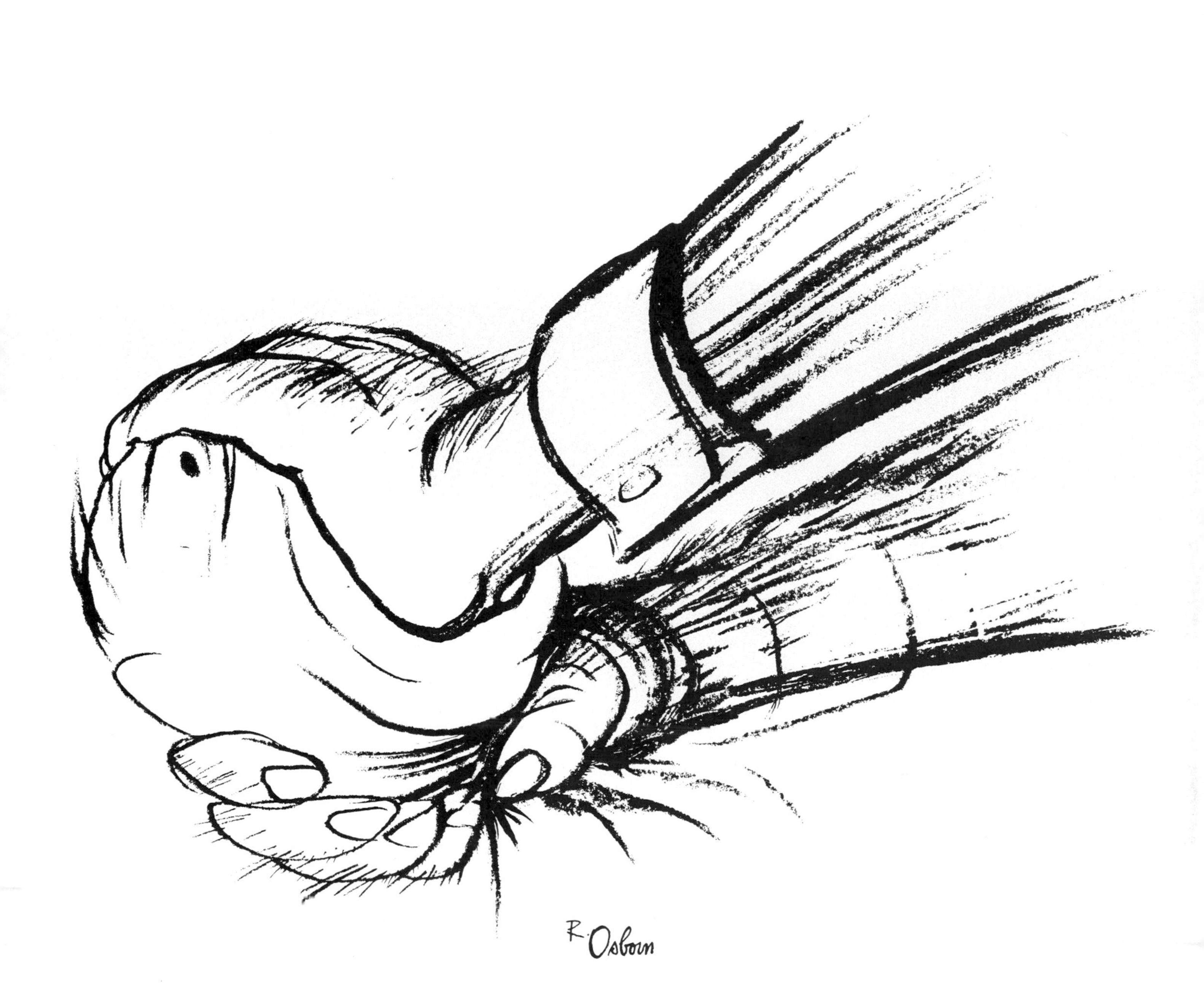

"If You Differ With Me We Will Silence You"
by Robert Osborn, 1954
Library of Congress, Prints and Photographs Division
Reprinted through the courtesy of Robert Osborn

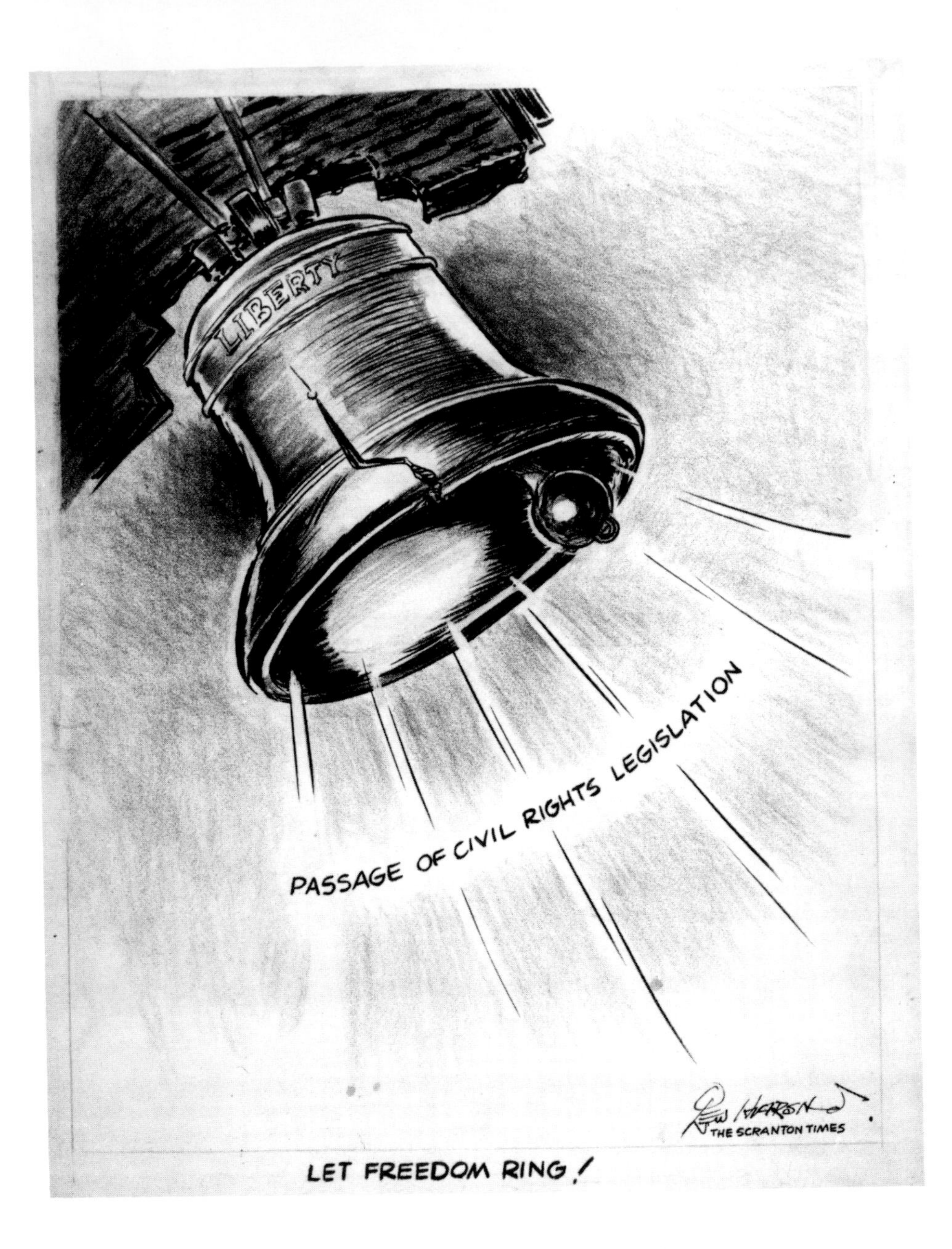

"Let Freedom Ring!"
by Lew Harsh, appeared in the *Scranton Times*, not dated
Lyndon Baines Johnson Library, National Archives
Reprinted through the courtesy of the *Scranton Times*

"Hang On, Kids — We're Decelerating"
by Bill Mauldin, appeared in the *Chicago Sun-Times*, 1969
Collection of Bill Mauldin
Reprinted with permission of Bill Mauldin

CIVIL RIGHTS
Transforming a political ideal — equality under the law — into a political reality for all Americans has been one goal of the civil rights movement.

"HANG ON, KIDS—WE'RE DECELERATING."

"WELL, GIRLS, AT LEAST THE ONLY WAY WE CAN GO IS UP."

'Men, We've Got to Improve Our Image'

"Men, We've Got to Improve Our Image"
by Jon Kennedy, appeared in the *Arkansas Democrat*, 1960s
The State Historical Society of Missouri, Columbia
Reprinted through the courtesy of The State Historical Society of Missouri, Columbia, and the *Arkansas Democrat*

The Ku Klux Klan (KKK) was one of several secret societies that rose in the South in the wake of the Civil War. Klan members used violence and terrorism to prevent black people from exercising their political rights. During the early 1920s the KKK gained strength in an atmosphere of rampant intolerance of blacks, Jews, Catholics, immigrants, and foreigners. Rocked by scandals, the Klan's power had diminished by 1925, but the civil rights movement of the 1950s and 1960s revitalized the Klan's activities.

Cartoonists have used the white-hooded robes, worn by Klan members, as a powerful symbol of this organization.

"Well, Girls, At Least The Only Way We Can Go Is Up"
By Bill Mauldin, appeared in the *Chicago Sun-Times*, 1974
Gerald R. Ford Museum, National Archives
Reprinted with permission of Bill Mauldin

In 1972 Congress passed the Equal Rights Amendment (ERA), which stated that "Equality of Rights . . . shall not be denied by the United States or by any state on account of sex."

The Constitution requires that three-fourths of the states ratify an amendment before it becomes law. The ratification process sparked debates on the question across the country. The ERA did not become law because it lacked the required number of states for approval.

"A Cold Reception Everywhere"
by J. Keppler, appeared in *Puck*, 1889
Franklin D. Roosevelt Library, National Archives

At the time of this cartoon, temperance was still a local and state issue. In the early 20th century, it became the central issue of a national movement that culminated in 1920 in national prohibition.

"Paste This On Your Dashboard"
by Harold M. Talburt, Scripps-Howard News Service, December 19, 1959
John Fitzgerald Kennedy Library, National Archives

PROHIBITION

Alcoholic beverages have been a part of American social life since colonial times. For more than two centuries, Americans have debated the merits and hazards of alcohol and its effect on our medical, moral, and social health. These debates have raised a very basic question about what role, if any, the government should play in controlling the personal behavior of its citizens.

"Green Pastures"
by Walter J. Enright, *Evening World*, May 29, year not known
Herbert Hoover Library, National Archives

"Inflation!"
by Frank Interlandi, appeared in the *Los Angeles Times*, 1975
Gerald R. Ford Museum, National Archives
Reprinted through the courtesy of Frank Interlandi

"Passing the Economy Buck"
by Jack Jurden, *Wilmington News Journal*, January 1982
Reagan Presidential Materials Staff, National Archives
Reprinted through the courtesy of Jack Jurden and the *Wilmington News Journal*

"The Cash Register Chorus"
by Daniel Robert Fitzpatrick, appeared in the *St. Louis Post-Dispatch*, September 21, 1924
The State Historical Society of Missouri, Columbia
Reprinted through the courtesy of The State Historical Society of Missouri, Columbia

Calvin Coolidge was President from 1923 to 1929, the period preceding the Depression. He had tremendous faith in the private enterprise system and did not believe in government control of business. During this period, there was little government restriction on American business practices. As this cartoon suggests, his policies were very popular with the business community.

BOOM and BUST

The American government has always had a role in protecting and promoting the economy. Fiscal and budgetary programs have been widely debated by editors and cartoonists.

THE CASH REGISTER CHORUS.

OCT 29
DIES IRAE
NY STOCK EX
CURB

"Oct. 29. Dies Irae" [Day of Wrath]
by James Rosenberg, 1929
Philadelphia Museum of Art: Purchased: Lola Downin Peck Fund from the Carl and Laura Zigrosser Collection

The stock market crash of 1929 marked the beginning of the Great Depression. An atmosphere of fear and panic prevailed on Wall Street on October 29, when stockholders traded a record 16 million shares in an effort to get whatever price they could for their stock.

"While Washington makes up its mind what kind of relief it wants to give the suffering"
by John T. McCutcheon, appeared in the *Chicago Tribune*, February 3, 1931
Herbert Hoover Library, National Archives

THE GREAT DEPRESSION

During the Great Depression, the debates intensified as the government's programs became increasingly involved in more areas of human activity. Many Americans welcomed the government's response to the crisis, while others viewed the new programs as an unwanted intrusion into the private domain.

[Roosevelt at the Wheel of Ship Going from Depression to Recovery]
by Widhoff, not dated
Franklin D. Roosevelt Library, National Archives

"Come Along — We're Going To The Trans-Lux To Hiss Roosevelt"
by Peter Arno, appeared in the *New Yorker*, September 19, 1936
Franklin D. Roosevelt Library, National Archives
© Estate of Peter Arno

FIFTY-FIFTY

"Fifty-Fifty"
by Burt Thomas, appeared in the *Detroit News*, 1935
Franklin D. Roosevelt Library, National Archives
Reprinted through the courtesy of the *Detroit News*

While some Americans viewed Franklin D. Roosevelt as a savior, others opposed the relief programs he proposed. Much of the opposition to Roosevelt's programs came from the wealthy, as suggested in these cartoons.

"Come along. We're going to the Trans-Lux to hiss Roosevelt."

President Reagan — Like a political cartoonist, your sense of humor may occasionally get you in trouble, but it's also one of your great strengths as a leader. — Respectfully, David Horsey

"It May Only Be Voodoo Economics, But You Must Admit It's Quite A Show!"
by David Horsey, appeared in the *Seattle Post-Intelligencer*, 1984
Reagan Presidential Materials Staff, National Archives
Reprinted through the courtesy of David Horsey and the *Seattle Post-Intelligencer*

During the 1980 Presidential primaries, Ronald Reagan promised to lower taxes, balance the budget, and increase defense spending. George Bush, then one of Reagan's opponents for the nomination, denounced these policies as "voodoo economics."

SOUNDS OF MUTINY ON THE BOUNTY.

3/23/60

"Sounds of Mutiny on the Bounty"
by Harold M. Talburt, Scripps-Howard News Service, March 23, 1960
John Fitzgerald Kennedy Library, National Archives

"Easy, Ol' Girl! I'm a Farm Boy, Remember? . . . I Know What I'm Doing . . ."
by Jeff MacNelly, appeared in the *Richmond News Leader*, September 1976
Gerald R. Ford Museum, National Archives
Reprinted through the courtesy of Jeff MacNelly

Government policies regarding the economy continue to be the subject of intense debate.

"Sees All—Knows All!"
by Fred Graf, appeared in the *Nassau Daily Review*, March 8, 1949
Still Picture Branch, National Archives

INTERNAL SECURITY

While the people of the United States have the right to protect their individual liberties, the government has the right to protect itself. One challenge of a free society is to keep these two principles in balance. At various times in our history, concerns for national security have prevailed over concerns for individual liberties.

"Trial Behind The Iron Curtain"
by Daniel Robert Fitzpatrick, appeared in the *St. Louis Post-Dispatch*, July 7, 1951
Victoria Schuck Collection at the John Fitzgerald Kennedy Library, National Archives
Fitzpatrick in the *St. Louis Post-Dispatch*

"Maypole Dance"
by Rube Goldberg, appeared in the *New York Journal-American*, May 1, 1958
Still Picture Branch, National Archives
Reprinted through the courtesy of King Features Syndicate, Inc.

RED SCARE, POST–WORLD WAR II

As the Soviet Union expanded into Eastern Europe following World War II, many Americans began to fear communist infiltration in the American government. During the 1950s communism and the Soviet Union became the embodiments of cruelty and suppression.

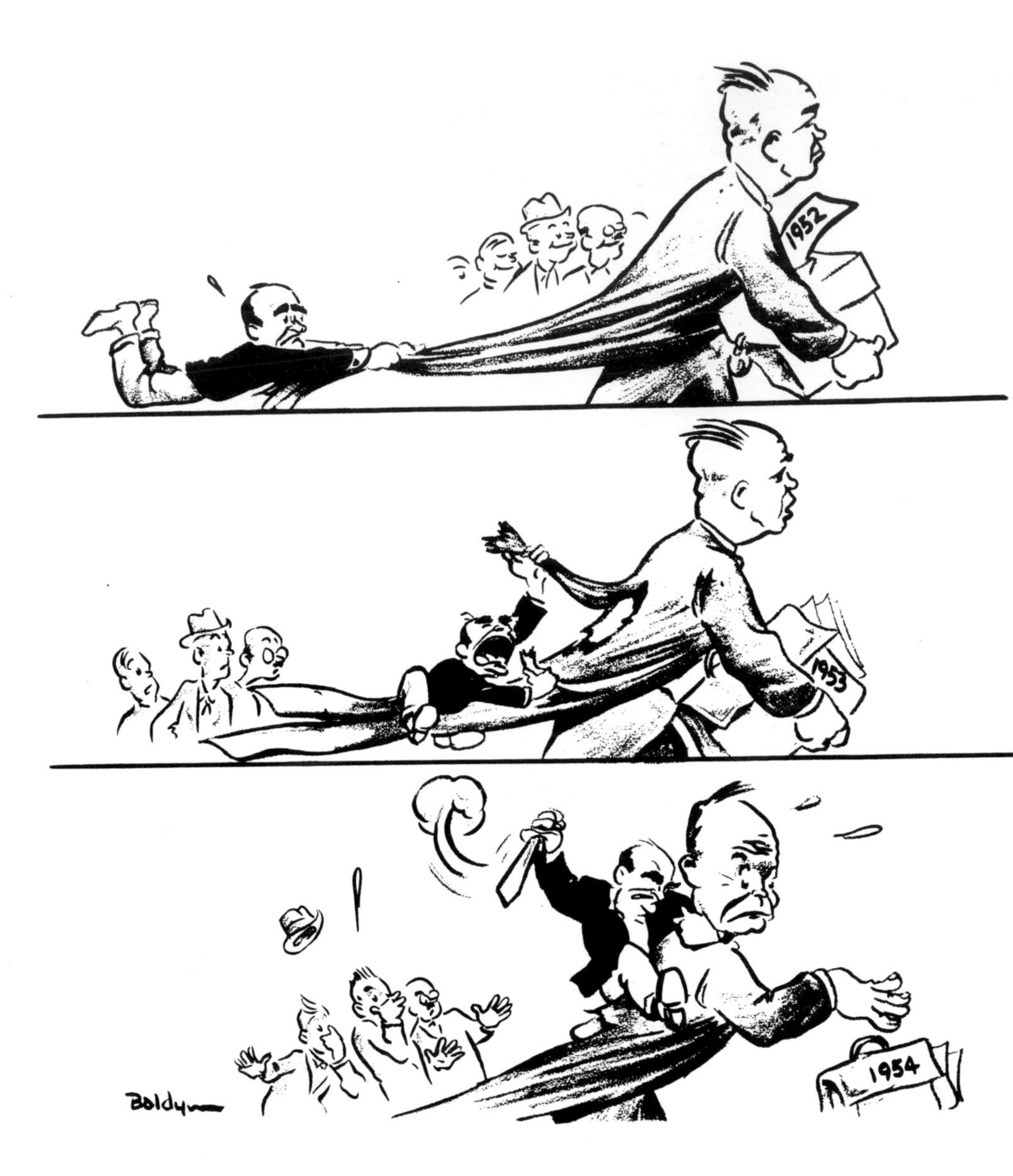

"The McCarthy Story"
by Clifford "Baldy" Baldowski, appeared in the *Atlanta Constitution*, ca. 1954
Dwight D. Eisenhower Library, National Archives
Reprinted through the courtesy of Clifford "Baldy" Baldowski and the *Atlanta Constitution*

This three-part drawing reflects the widening rift between the Eisenhower administration and the Republican right as McCarthyism ran its course during the early 1950s.

"The Difference Is, Our Cases Couldn't Be Reversed"
by Daniel Robert Fitzpatrick, appeared in the St. Louis *Post-Dispatch*, September 14, 1955
Victoria Schuck Collection at the John Fitzgerald Kennedy Library, National Archives
Fitzpatrick in the St. Louis *Post-Dispatch*

In 1950 Senator Joseph McCarthy exploited the fear of communist subversion, tainting the reputations of writers, performers, scholars, and other public figures with accusations of communist subversion. McCarthy's charges of disloyalty intimidated many Americans into silence. The efforts to root out communists were called witch hunts, in reference to the Salem witch hunts of 1692.

"THE DIFFERENCE IS, OUR CASES COULDN'T BE REVERSED"

ANARCHY
TREASON
DRAFT-CARD BURNINGS
AID AND COMFORT

"Aid and Comfort"
by Bob Taylor, appeared in the *Dallas Times-Herald*, October 19, 1965
Lyndon Baines Johnson Library, National Archives
Reprinted through the courtesy of the *Dallas Times-Herald*

"A Look Behind the Woodwork"
by Jack Knox, appeared in the *Nashville Banner*, January 6, 1968
Still Picture Branch, National Archives
Reprinted through the courtesy of Jack Knox and the *Nashville Banner*

Some people viewed the social unrest of the 1960s as the undoing of American society. They associated antiwar protests and the black power movement with anti-Americanism.

PRIVACY

The privacy of individuals can be a casualty of the government's campaign to protect itself against domestic threats. Cartoonists reflect a range of opinions regarding the government's efforts to search out disloyalty.

"'And You Assure Me, Colby, That the CIA Has Stopped All of Its Domestic Spying'"
by Ed Gamble, appeared in the *Nashville Banner*, 1974
Gerald R. Ford Museum, National Archives
Reprinted through the courtesy of Ed Gamble and the *Nashville Banner*

"Loyalty Check Up"
by Clifford K. Berryman, appeared in the *Washington Evening Star*, August 20, 1947
Still Picture Branch, National Archives
© 1947 *The Washington Post*, reprinted with permission.

[Peanuts Comic Strip—"Did You Ever Notice All the Tiny Lines on Your Fingers?"]
by Charles Schulz, United Feature Syndicate, Inc., August 2, 1954
Still Picture Branch, National Archives
© 1954 United Feature Syndicate, Inc.

"Crimony Folks, Enough Already! You Aren't Supposed to Read the Thing. You're Supposed to Look at It."
by David Catrow, appeared in the *Springfield News-Sun*, 1990
Collection of David Catrow
Reprinted through the courtesy of the *Springfield News-Sun*, Copley News Service

PARTING SHOT

Even the National Archives has provided grist for the cartoonists' mill. While waiting in line to view the Constitution at the National Archives, cartoonist David Catrow was inspired to draw this cartoon.

CHECKLIST

Titles appearing in quotes are taken directly from the cartoon; brackets around titles indicate editorial authorship. Dimensions are given in inches; height precedes width. Archival citations are given, as appropriate. The general headings and the sequence of the cartoons reflect the organization of the exhibition.

CARTOONIST'S STUDIO

"Alright You Editorial Cartoonists, DRAW!!"
by Jack Jurden, appeared in the *Wilmington News Journal*, May 29, 1971
India ink over purple pencil on paper
25¾ x 12
Lyndon Baines Johnson Library [73.1.998], National Archives

"A Brave Man"
by Cy Hungerford, appeared in the *Pittsburgh Post-Gazette*, not dated
India ink on paper
17 1/16 x 13¼
Lyndon Baines Johnson Library [73.1.2192], National Archives

"President Hoover Gets a Great Kick Out of His Cartoon Collection"
by Clifford K. Berryman, appeared in the *Washington Evening Star*, October 1932
India ink on paper
12¾ x 13⅞
Herbert Hoover Library [62.2.263], National Archives

"We've Grown Accustomed To Your Face"
by Frank Tyger, appeared in the *Trenton Times*, not dated
Felt tip pen and india ink with applied halftone film on artist's board
11⅜ x 11
Lyndon Baines Johnson Library [73.1.2694], National Archives

"Gee . . . I Feel Like I Understand Those Cartoonists Much Better Now. . . . Somebody Count the Silverware"
by Jim Borgman, the *Cincinnati Enquirer*, 1986
India ink, felt tip pen, colored markers, and colored chalk on artist's board
9 x 12
Reagan Presidential Materials Staff [8692510], National Archives

[Composite Caricature of Dwight D. Eisenhower]
by Milton Caniff, Carl Rose, Rube Goldberg, Russell Patterson, Mel Casson, Pierotti, and an unknown cartoonist, not dated
Fixed charcoal on artist's board
38½ x 26¾
Dwight D. Eisenhower Library [61-605], National Archives

INTRODUCTION

"Sounds of Mutiny on the Bounty"
by Harold M. Talburt, Scripps-Howard News Service, March 23, 1960
Pencil and india ink on coquille paper
15⅞ x 13⅜
John Fitzgerald Kennedy Library, National Archives

"Will You Love Me In December Like You Do In May?"
by Bill Mauldin, appeared in the *Chicago Sun-Times*, 1964
Ink, crayon, and opaque white on paper
13 13/16 x 10⅜
Lyndon Baines Johnson Library [65.28.387], National Archives

"If You Differ With Me We Will Silence You"
by Robert Osborn, 1954
Ink and crayon on paper
15 x 21
Library of Congress, Prints and Photographs Division

[Peanuts Comic Strip — "Did You Ever Notice All the Tiny Lines on Your Fingers?"]
by Charles Schulz, United Feature Syndicate, Inc., August 2, 1954
India ink over pencil on paper
Approximately 11 x 14
Still Picture Branch [65-HCA-54A], National Archives

"That Man in the White House"
by Robert Zschiesche, appeared in the *Greensboro Daily News*, September 7, 1967
India ink and crayon with opaque white on duoshade paper
13⅛ x 10⅞
Lyndon Baines Johnson Library [73.1.2217], National Archives

"The Harried Piano Player"
by Joseph Parrish, appeared in the *Chicago Tribune*, 1948
India ink and watercolor over pencil on paper
12⅞ x 13⅛
Harry S. Truman Library [85.290.2], National Archives

"Et Tu, Y'All?"
by Ken Alexander, appeared in the *San Francisco Examiner*, 1960s
India ink over pencil with applied halftone film on artist's board
13⅞ x 11
Lyndon Baines Johnson Library [73.1.305], National Archives

WAR AND PEACE

"Come On In, I'll Treat You Right. I Used To Know Your Daddy"
by C. D. Batchelor, appeared in the *New York Daily News*, April 25, 1936
Ink and pencil on paper
21 x 14
Pulitzer Prize Collection, Columbia University

World War II

"The Misfit"
by Edwin Marcus, appeared in the *New York Times*, 1933
India ink on artist's board
14 x 13½
Library of Congress, Prints and Photographs Division

"Another Good Soldier"
by Rube Goldberg, King Features Syndicate, Inc., March 9, 1942
India ink and crayon on paper
19¾ x 15½
Franklin D. Roosevelt Library [MO88-1:65], National Archives

"A Tree Grows in Berlin"
by Daniel Robert Fitzpatrick, appeared in the *St. Louis Post-Dispatch*, August 17, 1944
Crayon, india ink, and opaque white on paper
23½ x 20
Victoria Schuck Collection at the John Fitzgerald Kennedy Library, National Archives

"The Harvest"
by Daniel Robert Fitzpatrick, appeared in the *St. Louis Post-Dispatch*, November 27, 1938
Crayon, india ink, and opaque white on paper
23½ x 20⅜
Victoria Schuck Collection at the John Fitzgerald Kennedy Library, National Archives

"Who's Pearl Harbor?"
by Lee Judge, appeared in the *Kansas City Times*, August 7, 1985
India ink and red pencil on duoshade artist's board
9 11/16 x 8¼
Harry S. Truman Library [85.284.1], National Archives

"'Fresh, spirited American troops, flushed with victory, are bringing in thousands of hungry, ragged, battle-weary prisoners . . .' (News Item)"
by Bill Mauldin, United Feature Syndicate, Inc., 1944
India ink over pencil on paper
10¾ x 8
Pulitzer Prize Collection, Columbia University

"Class of '45"
by Bill Mauldin, October 16, 1967
India ink on paper
10 3/16 x 7⅜
Dwight D. Eisenhower Library [70-372], National Archives

"The Sad Sack — Mechanized War"
by Sgt. George Baker, appeared in *Yank*, not dated
Reproduction
Dwight D. Eisenhower Library [79-183.3], National Archives

"The Sad Sack — Planning"
by Sgt. George Baker, appeared in *Yank*, not dated
Reproduction
Dwight D. Eisenhower Library [79-183.1], National Archives

"Down to Bottomless Perdition"
by Daniel Robert Fitzpatrick, appeared in the *St. Louis Post-Dispatch*, May 7, 1945
Crayon, india ink, and opaque white on paper
21 x 18 1/4
Victoria Schuck Collection at the John Fitzgerald Kennedy Library, National Archives

Post–World War II

"The Shape of Things Now"
by Daniel Robert Fitzpatrick, appeared in the *St. Louis Post-Dispatch*, March 4, 1945
Crayon, india ink, and opaque white on paper
21 7/16 X 18 5/16
Victoria Schuck Collection at the John Fitzgerald Kennedy Library, National Archives

"Hands Across the Sea"
by Dougal Rodger, probably appeared in the *San Francisco News*, not dated
Reproduction
Harry S. Truman Library [77.97.99.6], National Archives

"History Repeats"
by Vincent A. Svoboda, appeared in the *Brooklyn Eagle*, 1946
Pencil on paper
13 1/8 x 11 1/4
Herbert Hoover Library [62.1.648], National Archives

"Their Tearjerker"
by Joseph Parrish, appeared in the *Chicago Tribune*, 1946
India ink over pencil on artist's board
12 x 12 1/4
Harry S. Truman Library [85.290.30], National Archives

Vietnam War

". . . Meanwhile, Back on the Home Front"
by Gene Basset, Scripps-Howard News Service, November 1, 1965
Ink and crayon on paper
13 11/16 x 11 1/2
Lyndon Baines Johnson Library [65.28.25], National Archives

"Speaking of War Crimes"
by Edmund Valtman, appeared in the *Hartford Times*, October 2, 1965
India ink on duoshade artist's board
14 3/16 x 11 1/4
Lyndon Baines Johnson Library [73.1.2976], National Archives

"How Deep You Figure We'll Get Involved, Sir!"
by Bil Canfield, appeared in the *Newark (NJ) Star-Ledger*, not dated
India ink and crayon over blue pencil with opaque white on artist's board
15 7/8 x 17 3/8
National Press Club Collection, Washington, DC

"I Wear It Where I Need It"
by Bill Mauldin, appeared in the *Chicago Sun-Times*, May 21, 1965
Ink and crayon on paper
14 x 11
Lyndon Baines Johnson Library [65.28.398], National Archives

"There's A War On?"
by Warren King, appeared in the *New York Daily News*, 1966
Ink and crayon
22 1/4 16 13/16
Lyndon Baines Johnson Library [66.64.201], National Archives

[LBJ and Vietnam Specters]
by J. Paul Szep, appeared in the *Boston Globe*, 1960s
Black ink on artist's board
14 1/2 x 14
Library of Congress, Prints and Photographs Division

"He Was Talking about Vietnam and Then — "
by Bruce Shanks, appeared in the *Buffalo Evening News*, April 1, 1968
Ink, crayon, and opaque white on paper
17 x 14
Lyndon Baines Johnson Library [73.1.476], National Archives

Post–Vietnam War

"Pick Up Your Checks At The Rear Door. This Entrance Is For Real Veterans."
by Oliphant, appeared in the *Denver Post*, April 24, 1974
India ink on duoshade artist's board
11 3/4 x 17 1/2
Susan Conway Carroll Gallery, Washington, DC

"Chill In The Room"
by Bert Whitman, appeared in the *Phoenix Gazette*, January 7, 1977
India ink, crayon, and opaque white on coquille board
11 1/2 x 17 1/2
Jimmy Carter Library [77.284.9], National Archives

The Nuclear Era

"Hiroshima"
by Robert Osborn, 1945
Crayon and pencil on paper
13 1/4 x 10
Library of Congress, Prints and Photographs Division

"Say That H-Bomb Is Dangerous"
by Herbert Block ("Herblock"), appeared in the *Washington Post*, 1954
Ink, pencil, and opaque white on paper
19 1/4 x 14 3/8
Herbert Hoover Library [75.1.4], National Archives

"It's a LADY!"
by Bob Stevens, Copley Newspapers, March 28, 1967
India ink, crayon, and opaque white on paper
14 1/2 x 9 3/4
Lyndon Baines Johnson Library [73.1.1822], National Archives

"War!! My God!! It's the End of Us!!"
by Alexander Hunter, appeared in the *Washington Times*, 1984
India ink and felt tip pen with opaque white on paper
13 1/2 x 16 1/2
Reagan Presidential Materials Staff [8401787], National Archives

[Long-Distance View of the Arms Race]
by Tony Auth, appeared in the *Philadelphia Inquirer*, November 15, 1978
India ink over blue pencil on duoshade artist's board
10 13/16 x 14 7/8
National Press Club Collection, Washington, DC

POLITICAL CORRUPTION

"Who Stole the People's Money? Do Tell. 'Twas Him"
by Thomas Nast, appeared in *Harper's Weekly*, August 17, 1871
Wood engraving
15 5/8 x 11
Office of Public Programs, National Archives

"The Tammany Tiger Loose, What Are You Going To Do About It?"
by Thomas Nast, appeared in *Harper's Weekly*, November 11, 1871
Wood engraving
22 x 15 5/8
Office of Public Programs, National Archives

"Can the Law Reach Him?"
by Thomas Nast, appeared in *Harper's Weekly*, January 6, 1872
Wood engraving
15 3/4 x 10 11/16
Office of Public Programs, National Archives

"Washington Bomb"
by Daniel Robert Fitzpatrick, appeared in the *St. Louis Post-Dispatch*, January 1942
Crayon and india ink over charcoal with opaque white on paper
21 5/16 x 18
Harry S. Truman Library [2828], National Archives

"If This Thing Grows Much Bigger I May Have To Drop It"
by John C. Conacher, 1924
India ink and scraping out on artist's board
14 x 11 1/2
Library of Congress, Prints and Photographs Division

"Watergate Shoot-Out"
by Edward Sorel, appeared in *Ramparts*, June 1972
Watercolor, tempera, and india ink on paper
19 3/8 x 23 3/4
Collection of Byron Dobell

"I Have Discovered That According to a Secret Tape of June 23, 1972, I *Am* a Crook"
by Bill Sanders, appeared in the *Milwaukee Journal*, August 6, 1974
India ink over blue pencil on duoshade artist's board
14 x 11 1/4
National Press Club Collection, Washington, DC

"Really! Spiro!"
by Lou Grant, appeared in the *Oakland Tribune*, 1973
Ink and crayon on paper
11 x 8 1/2
Collection of Lou Grant

"As A Matter Of Fact I *Do* Work for H.U.D. . . . Why Do You Ask? . . .
by Walt Handelsman, appeared in the *Scranton Times*, 1989
Reproduction
Collection of Walt Handelsman

PRESIDENTIAL CARICATURES

"George Bush"
by Oliphant
Bronze, 1989
26 1/2 x 39 x 11
Susan Conway Carroll Gallery, Washington, DC

"The More Things Change The More They Stay The Same"
by Edmund Valtman, appeared in the *White Plains* (NY) *Dispatch*, January 2, 1969
India ink over pencil with applied half-tone film on paper
14 3/16 x 11 1/4
Still Picture Branch [65-HC-20-8], National Archives

Theodore Roosevelt

"A Bugle Call . . ."
by Thomas Nast
India ink, pencil, gouache, and crayon on artist's board
21 3/16 x 14 7/16
Franklin D. Roosevelt Library [MO90-15:1], National Archives

Herbert Hoover

[Hunger Attacks the American Home]
by G. W. Reinbold, appeared in the *Williamsport* (PA) *Grit*, July 8, 1917
India ink on paper
18 5/8 x 14 1/8
Herbert Hoover Library [62.1.641], National Archives

"It's going to be universal training for these, anyway"
by Jay Norwood "Ding" Darling, appeared in the *Des Moines Register and Leader*, 1917
India ink on paper
21 5/8 x 27 5/8
Herbert Hoover Library [62.3.7], National Archives

"How Will Hoover Go Down in History?"
by Jay Norwood "Ding" Darling, appeared in the *Des Moines Register and Leader*, August 26, 1929
India ink over pencil on artist's board
28 5/8 x 22 9/16
Herbert Hoover Library [87.9], National Archives

Franklin D. Roosevelt

[Caricature of Franklin D. Roosevelt]
by Eugene Alenquist, not dated
Pencil, crayon, and watercolor on paper
15 1/4 x 9 7/8
Franklin D. Roosevelt Library [52-430], National Archives

[President Franklin D. Roosevelt Leading His People Out of the Chaos of the Depression]
by Alexander Cochrane, not dated
India ink on paper
15 1/4 x 11 3/16
Franklin D. Roosevelt Library [MO84-29], National Archives

[President Franklin D. Roosevelt's Cigarette Holder]
by Art Randel, 1945
Charcoal and watercolor on artist's board
15 1/2 x 20 1/4
Franklin D. Roosevelt Library [MO74-287], National Archives

Harry S. Truman

"Time Flies — And So Does Harry"
by Cy Hungerford, appeared in the *Pittsburgh Post-Gazette*, April 1950
India ink over pencil with opaque white on paper
13 1/2 x 12 7/8
Harry S. Truman Library [2899], National Archives

[Caricature of Harry S. Truman]
by Otto Soglow, from volume of sketches of President Truman made by members of the National Cartoonist Society, presented to the President on October 3, 1949
Black crayon on paper
13 1/2 x 10 1/2
Harry S. Truman Library [70.124.12], National Archives

"See What You Can Do About Digging Up a Piano . . ."
by Oliphant, appeared in the *Denver Post*, 1972
India ink and applied caption on duoshade artist's board
11 9/16 x 17 5/8
Harry S. Truman Library [73.54.1], National Archives

Dwight D. Eisenhower

"Infectious"
by Joseph Parrish, appeared in the *Chicago Tribune*, 1955
India ink on paper
17 x 14 1/2
Dwight D. Eisenhower Library [56-165], National Archives

John F. Kennedy

"But You Aren't Jackie And I'm Not The President And This Ain't The White House!"
by Frank Miller, appeared in the *Des Moines Register and Tribune*, April 1963
India ink on paper
18 x 13 1/4
John Fitzgerald Kennedy Library [FI 102], National Archives

"The New Look"
by Art Wood, appeared in the *Pittsburgh Press*, February 8, 1960
Ink, pencil, and opaque white on paper
14 3/4 x 11
John Fitzgerald Kennedy Library, National Archives

[Lincoln Mourning the Death of President Kennedy]
by Bill Mauldin, appeared in the *Chicago Sun-Times*, November 22, 1963
Ink and crayon on paper
Approximately 18 x 14 5/8
John Fitzgerald Kennedy Library, National Archives

[Once There Was A Sleeping Country]
by Jules Feiffer, January 5, 1964
India ink with opaque white on paper
14 1/2 x 23
John Fitzgerald Kennedy Library, National Archives

Lyndon B. Johnson

[LBJ and Two Cherubs: Domestic Policy, Foreign Policy]
by Bob Taylor, appeared in the *Dallas Times-Herald*, January 13, 1965
India ink and crayon on paper
$12\frac{13}{16} \times 10\frac{3}{4}$
Lyndon Baines Johnson Library [73.1.799],
National Archives

"Lyndon Enlightening the World"
by Fred O. Seibel, appeared in the *Richmond Times-Dispatch*, October 5, 1965
India ink on paper
$18\frac{3}{16} \times 15$
Lyndon Baines Johnson Library [73.1.428],
National Archives

[LBJ Showing His Scar, Shaped Like a Map of Vietnam]
by David Levine, appeared in the *New York Review of Books*, 1966
Reproduction
Lyndon Baines Johnson Library [87.32.1],
National Archives

[Horse Without a Rider]
by Paul Conrad, appeared in the *Los Angeles Times*, January 1973
India ink and crayon on paper
$13\frac{7}{8} \times 11\frac{1}{8}$
Lyndon Baines Johnson Library [73.1.2590],
National Archives

Richard M. Nixon

[Caricature of President Nixon in Prison Stripes Chained to the "Press"]
by Jeff MacNelly, appeared in the *Richmond News Leader*, not dated
India ink over pencil on duoshade artist's board
$11 \times 15\frac{5}{16}$
National Press Club Collection,
Washington, DC

"The Smoking Gun"
by Oliphant, 1984
Lithograph
$26\frac{1}{2} \times 22$
Susan Conway Carroll Gallery,
Washington, DC

Gerald R. Ford

"Gentlemen, We're Supposed To Be Protecting Our Chief"
by Bill Roberts, appeared in the *Cleveland Press*, Scripps-Howard News Service, November 10, 1975
India ink over pencil with felt tip pen captions on duoshade artist's board
$12 \times 17\frac{5}{8}$
Gerald R. Ford Museum [988.394/72],
National Archives

Jimmy Carter

[Peanut Caricature of Jimmy Carter]
by Tom Curtis, appeared in the *Milwaukee Sentinel*, January 20, 1977
India ink over blue pencil on duoshade artist's board
$10 \times 14\frac{1}{8}$
Jimmy Carter Library [77.283.1],
National Archives

"'Well, I'll Be A Fiddle Stompin', Goose Hollerin' Son Of A Gun. . . . Lookie Thar, Jimmy! There's Old Fred Stumps From Plains. . . . Hey . . . Come On Up Here, Fred, And Have A Beer . . .!'"
by Ed Gamble, appeared in the *Nashville Banner*, 1977
India ink over blue pencil on duoshade artist's board
$12 \times 15\frac{3}{16}$
Jimmy Carter Library [77.287.3],
National Archives

Ronald Reagan

"Let 'em eat cake"
by David Levine, 1981
India ink on paper
14×11
Library of Congress, Prints and Photographs Division

"Sir . . . Do You Think You're Too Old To Run? Sure My Old Movies Were Fun . . ."
by Mike Peters, appeared in the *Dayton Daily News*, 1984
India ink, felt tip pen with opaque white on paper
$11\frac{5}{8} \times 15$
Collection of Mike Peters

A SCENE FROM THE NATIONAL ARCHIVES

"Crimony Folks, Enough Already! You Aren't Supposed to Read the Thing. You're Supposed to Look at It."
by David Catrow, appeared in the *Springfield News-Sun*, Copley News Service, 1990
India ink on paper
$9 \times 13\frac{1}{4}$
Collection of David Catrow

RACE FOR THE WHITE HOUSE

[Franklin D. Roosevelt and Herbert Hoover]
by Peter Arno, cover of the *New Yorker*, March 4, 1933
Magazine cover, not circulated
$11\frac{7}{8} \times 8\frac{11}{16}$
Franklin D. Roosevelt Library [MO56-345],
National Archives

"The Sphinx — 1940 Model"
by Leo Joseph Roche, appeared in the *Buffalo Courier Express*, November 16, 1939
India ink, crayon, and opaque white on paper
$18\frac{1}{8} \times 14\frac{1}{4}$
Franklin D. Roosevelt Library [MO74-285],
National Archives

"I Want Y'All"
by Blaine, appeared in the *Hamilton Spectator* (Ontario, Canada), 1964
India ink over pencil on artist's board
$15\frac{1}{4} \times 13\frac{3}{4}$
Lyndon Baines Johnson Library [73.1.487],
National Archives

[Candidates Kennedy and Nixon Approach Performers' Entrance to National TV Studio]
by Bill Sanders, appeared in the *Greensboro Daily News*, October 1960
India ink over pencil with opaque white on coquille paper
$18\frac{1}{4} \times 14\frac{1}{8}$
John Fitzgerald Kennedy Library,
National Archives

"Two Responses to Country's Call"
by Thomas Nast, 1892
India ink and opaque white on artist's board
28×22
Franklin D. Roosevelt Library [MO90-15:2],
National Archives

"Where Was Dan?"
by Jim Morin, appeared in the *Miami Herald*, August 19, 1988
India ink over pencil with opaque white on paper
11×17
Collection of Jim Morin

"No Place for a Kiddie Car"
by Daniel Robert Fitzpatrick, appeared in the *St. Louis Post-Dispatch*, March 29, 1940
India ink and crayon with opaque white on paper
$19\frac{1}{2} \times 17$
Harry S. Truman Library [1030],
National Archives

"Hi — My Name's Jimmy Carter — I Told You So!"
by Bill Garner, appeared in the *Commercial Appeal*, 1977
India ink and felt tip pen with opaque white on artist's board
$8\frac{1}{4} \times 11\frac{1}{16}$
Jimmy Carter Library [77.297.2],
National Archives

BALANCE OF POWER

"The Balance of Power"
by Burris Jenkins, Jr., appeared in the *New York World Telegram*, April 1952
Crayon, charcoal, and ink on paper
$14\frac{1}{2} \times 11\frac{1}{2}$
Harry S. Truman Library [2166],
National Archives

The Executive and the Legislature

"Another Boundary Dispute!"
by Walter J. Enright, appeared in the *Evening World*, ca. 1929–30
Crayon over blue pencil on coquille paper
$18\frac{3}{4} \times 14\frac{1}{4}$
Herbert Hoover Library [62.8.22],
National Archives

"The Lightning Speed of Honesty"
by Thomas Nast, appeared in *Harper's Weekly*, November 24, 1877
Wood engraving
15⅝ x 11
Office of Public Programs, National Archives

"The Galloping Snail"
by Burt Thomas, appeared in the *Detroit News*, ca. March 20, 1933
Ink and pencil on paper
14⅛ x 13½
Franklin D. Roosevelt Library [MO56-396], National Archives

"And When Did You First Notice We Weren't Listening?"
by Hy Rosen, appeared in the *Albany Times Union*, April 13, 1975
India ink on duoshade artist's board
11½ x 15½
Gerald R. Ford Museum [987.294/1], National Archives

"A Presidential Touch"
by Cy Hungerford, appeared in the *Pittsburgh Post-Gazette*, January 17, 1957
India ink on paper
16⅞ x 13¼
Dwight D. Eisenhower Library [57-290.1], National Archives

"Frankly, Scarletface — Ah don't give dams . . ."
by Corky Trinidad, appeared in the *Honolulu Star-Bulletin*, 1977
India ink over blue pencil on duoshade artist's board
11 x 15⅛
Jimmy Carter Library [77.288.2], National Archives

The Executive and the Judiciary

"Modern Crucifixion — by the Nine Ancients — 1935 A.D."
by Harry S. Outhwaite, 1935
Pencil on paper
23⅞ x 17⅞
Franklin D. Roosevelt Library [MO83-5:1], National Archives

"New Deal Plan for Enlarged Supreme Court"
by Clifford K. Berryman, appeared in the *Washington Evening Star*, February 10, 1937
Ink on paper
13½ x 14½
Library of Congress, Prints and Photographs Division

The Imperial Presidency

"King George IV"
by Paul Conrad, appeared in the *Los Angeles Times*, December 1990
India ink on artist's board
10 x 8⅜
Collection of Paul Conrad

"Milhous I"
by Edward Sorel, appeared in *Rolling Stone*, March 14, 1974
Reproduction
Library of Congress, Prints and Photographs Division

"History's Burlesque"
by Joseph Parrish, appeared in the *Chicago Tribune*, 1949
India ink on artist's board
13⅞ x 13⅛
Harry S. Truman Library [85.290.36], National Archives

The Drama of Executive Staffing

[Doonesbury Strip — "Jerry, I've Been Meaning To Talk To You For Some Time"]
by Garry Trudeau, Universal Press Syndicate, June 24, 1974
India ink over pencil with opaque white on paper
10¼ x 22⅛
Gerald R. Ford Museum [988.546/1], National Archives

"White House Solitaire"
by Franklin O. Alexander, appeared in the *Philadelphia Evening Bulletin*, September 23, 1966
India ink and crayon on paper
13 x 11⅜
Lyndon Baines Johnson Library [73.1.2147], National Archives

"Reveille"
by Herbert Block, ("Herblock"), appeared in the *Washington Post*, 1951
India ink on paper
20⅜ x 14¼
Harry S. Truman Library [1136], National Archives

"I Don't Think Much of MacArthur Meself"
by Bill Mauldin, not dated
Crayon on paper
16½ x 13¾
Harry S. Truman Library [2267], National Archives

DOMESTIC ISSUES

"Bell-Ringer"
by Herbert Block ("Herblock"), appeared in the *Washington Post*, 1948
India ink and pencil with opaque white on coquille paper
17⅛ x 13¼
Harry S. Truman Library [1128], National Archives

"Let Freedom Ring!"
by Lew Harsh, appeared in the *Scranton Times*, not dated
India ink, crayon, and opaque white on coquille paper
18⅛ x 14⅛
Lyndon Baines Johnson Library [73.1.406], National Archives

Civil Rights

"The Bright Sun Casts a Black Shadow"
by Thomas Nast, 1892
India ink and pencil on paper
14 x 10¹⁵⁄₁₆
Franklin D. Roosevelt Library [MO90-15:3], National Archives

"Men, We've Got to Improve Our Image"
by Jon Kennedy, appeared in the *Arkansas Democrat*, 1960s
Ink and pencil on paper
13¾ x 10¹¹⁄₁₆
The State Historical Society of Missouri, Columbia

"Hang On, Kids — We're Decelerating"
by Bill Mauldin, appeared in the *Chicago Sun-Times*, 1969
Reproduction
Collection of Bill Mauldin

"Well, Girls, At Least the Only Way We Can Go Is Up"
by Bill Mauldin, appeared in the *Chicago Sun-Times*, 1974
India ink and crayon with opaque white on paper
11½ x 9½
Gerald R. Ford Museum [989.136/1], National Archives

Prohibition

"A Cold Reception Everywhere"
by J. Keppler, appeared in *Puck*, 1889
Color lithograph
13½ x 20¼
Franklin D. Roosevelt Library [43-73-5], National Archives

"Green Pastures"
by Walter J. Enright, *Evening World*, May 29, year not known
Crayon over blue pencil on coquille paper
22⅛ x 15³⁄₁₆
Herbert Hoover Library [62.8.21], National Archives

"Paste This On Your Dashboard"
by Harold M. Talburt, Scripps-Howard News Service, December 19, 1959
Pencil and opaque white on coquille paper
13⅛ x 11½
John Fitzgerald Kennedy Library, National Archives

Boom and Bust

"The Cash Register Chorus"
by Daniel Robert Fitzpatrick, appeared in the *St. Louis Post-Dispatch*, September 21, 1924
India ink, charcoal, and opaque white on paper
22 x 19½
The State Historical Society of Missouri, Columbia

"Oct. 29. Dies Irae" [Day of Wrath]
by James Rosenberg, 1929
Lithograph on colored paper
14⅞ x 11⅛
Philadelphia Museum of Art: Purchased: Lola Downin Peck Fund from the Carl and Laura Zigrosser Collection

"While Washington makes up its mind what kind of relief it wants to give the suffering"
by John T. McCutcheon, appeared in the *Chicago Tribune*, February 3, 1931
Ink on paper
18$^{9}/_{16}$ x 14⅛
Herbert Hoover Library [80.12.17], National Archives

[Republican Elephant Lifting the Drowned Public Out of the Sea of Depression]
by John Rhoads, Jr., not dated
India ink on artist's board
11 x 14
Herbert Hoover Library [62.2.40], National Archives

[Roosevelt at the Wheel of Ship Going from Depression to Recovery]
by Widhoff, not dated
India ink, crayon, and opaque white on paper
11½ x 14½
Franklin D. Roosevelt Library [43-58-6], National Archives

"Come Along—We're Going To The Trans-Lux To Hiss Roosevelt"
by Peter Arno, appeared in the *New Yorker*, September 19, 1936
Reproduction
Franklin D. Roosevelt Library [MO71-54], National Archives

"Fifty-Fifty"
by Burt Thomas, appeared in the *Detroit News*, 1935
Reproduction
Franklin D. Roosevelt Library [MO56-398], National Archives

"Passing the Economy Buck"
by Jack Jurden, *Wilmington News Journal*, January 1982
Reproduction
Reagan Presidential Materials Staff [8240175], National Archives

"Inflation!"
by Frank Interlandi, appeared in the *Los Angeles Times*, 1975
India ink over blue pencil with crayon on paper
11¼ x 9¼
Gerald R. Ford Museum [989.879/1], National Archives

"Easy, Ol' Girl! I'm a Farm Boy, Remember? . . . I Know What I'm Doing . . ."
by Jeff MacNelly, appeared in the *Richmond News Leader*, September 1976
India ink over pencil with opaque white on duoshade artist's board
10⅞ x 15$^{9}/_{16}$
Gerald R. Ford Museum [86.8/7], National Archives

"It May Only Be Voodoo Economics, But You Must Admit It's Quite A Show!"
by David Horsey, appeared in the *Seattle Post-Intelligencer*, 1984
India ink over pencil with opaque white on duoshade artist's paper
11½ x 17¾
Reagan Presidential Materials Staff [8601066], National Archives

Internal Security

"Maypole Dance"
by Rube Goldberg, appeared in the *New York Journal-American*, May 1, 1958
Black crayon, india ink, and opaque white on coquille paper
Approximately 18¼ x 15¼
Still Picture Branch [65-HCA-34B], National Archives

"Trial Behind The Iron Curtain"
by Daniel Robert Fitzpatrick, appeared in the *St. Louis Post-Dispatch*, July 7, 1951
Crayon, india ink, and opaque white on paper
21 x 17⅞
Victoria Schuck Collection at the John Fitzgerald Kennedy Library, National Archives

"The Difference Is, Our Cases Couldn't Be Reversed"
by Daniel Robert Fitzpatrick, appeared in the *St. Louis Post-Dispatch*, September 14, 1955
Crayon, india ink, and opaque white on paper
17⅞ x 14½
Victoria Schuck Collection at the John Fitzgerald Kennedy Library, National Archives

"The McCarthy Story"
by Clifford "Baldy" Baldowski, appeared in the *Atlanta Constitution*, ca. 1954
Pencil and india ink with opaque white on coquille paper
16⅞ x 13⅞
Dwight D. Eisenhower Library [65-174.1], National Archives

"A Look Behind the Woodwork"
by Jack Knox, appeared in the *Nashville Banner*, January 6, 1968
Crayon over blue pencil on coquille paper
Approximately 13¼ x 10¼
Still Picture Branch [65-HCA-9A], National Archives

"Aid and Comfort"
by Bob Taylor, appeared in the *Dallas Times-Herald*, October 19, 1965
India ink, pencil, crayon, and blue pencil on coquille paper
14⅛ x 11
Lyndon Baines Johnson Library [73.1.1901], National Archives

"Women's Lib"
by Gene Basset, Scripps-Howard News Service, not dated
India ink over pencil with opaque white on paper
14 x 10¼
Still Picture Branch [65-HC-9A-2], National Archives

"Sees All—Knows All!"
by Fred Graf, appeared in the *Nassau Daily Review*, March 8, 1949
India ink and crayon over blue pencil on coquille paper
12 x 9$^{3}/_{16}$
Still Picture Branch [65-HC-11-27], National Archives

"Loyalty Check Up"
by Clifford K. Berryman, appeared in the *Washington Evening Star*, August 20, 1947
India ink over pencil on paper
12⅞ x 13$^{15}/_{16}$
Still Picture Branch [65-HC-9A-14], National Archives

"'And You Assure Me, Colby, That the CIA Has Stopped All of Its Domestic Spying'"
by Ed Gamble, appeared in the *Nashville Banner*, 1974
India ink over pencil on duoshade artist's board
11¾ x 15¾
Gerald R. Ford Museum [81.204/8], National Archives

PARTING SHOTS

"Just Let Me Leave With My Dignity Intact"
by Ed Stein, appeared in the *Rocky Mountain News*, Newspaper Enterprise Alliance, 1989
India ink over pencil with opaque white on paper
9 x 12$^{1}/_{16}$
Collection of Ed Stein

***The Washington Post*, November 22, 1989, showing "The Pack Is Prologue"**
by Herbert Block ("Herblock")
Newspaper
23½ x 27⅝
Office of Public Programs, National Archives